TEN-SECOND
BUSINESS
FORMS

TEN-SECOND BUSINESS FORMS

3rd Edition

Robert L. Adams

BOB ADAMS, INC.
Holbrook, Massachusetts

Published by Bob Adams, Inc.
260 Center Street, Holbrook, MA 02343

ISBN: 1-55850-307-2

Printed in the United States of America

A   B   C   D   E   F   G   H   I   J

The author strongly recommends that all self-employed people and small business owners develop a strong relationship with a Certified Public Accountant, a lawyer experienced in small business law, and a commercial banker. These experts should be consulted regularly in the course of building your small business and will be able to offer you ideas on how to maximize the use of the forms in this book for your own business.

— *Robert L. Adams*

This publication is designed to provide accurate and authoritative information with regard to the subject matter covered. It is sold with the understanding that the publisher is not engaged in rendering legal, accounting, or other professional advice. If legal advice or other expert assistance is required, the services of a qualified professional person should be sought.

— From a *Declaration of Principles* jointly adopted by a Committee of the American Bar Association and a Committee of Publishers and Associations.

This book is available at quantity discounts for bulk purchases.
For information, call 1-800-872-5627.

Acknowledgments

My thanks for all their help to the following, without whom this book would not be the comprehensive business resource and overall small business management tool that it is: To Monique Avakian for her production work in producing many of the forms herein; to Eric Blume for helping with the cover design and concept; to Brandon Toropov for his overall help in coordinating this project; and most of all to Christopher Ciaschini for his tireless, often 'round-the-clock stints in producing the majority of forms in this book. I would also like to thank my Professors at The Harvard Business School who taught me many of the key business concepts behind the use and design of many of the forms in this book. Finally, I would like to thank my Father, who helped finance my business school education.

Contents

Introduction

Congratulations! You've just purchased a resource that will save you, your small business or your office time and money, and improve the image you project to your customers, suppliers, and employees.

You can begin to reap the benefits of TEN-SECOND BUSINESS FORMS immediately, by saving countless hours that would otherwise have been spent designing and assembling your own forms. And you may well find that the "payback period" on this book has been reached with your very first use. By photocopying a single batch of forms, your business will bypass the expenses, not only of design and production, but also of the costly delays that so often accompany jobs given to commercial printers.

However, this book is far more than a money- and time-saver. TEN-SECOND BUSINESS FORMS is an efficient management tool. The forms it contains will help you speed the collection of receivables, boost sales, track inventories, record expenses, organize workflow, evaluate job applicants, reduce phone costs, make credit decisions, evaluate payroll, prepare budgets and much more.

Perhaps most importantly, this book has been designed to yield years of use. Until now, business form books have either been of the self-destruct type (pages ripped out to lie flat on the copier) or saddle-stitched (in which one pounded the book in an unsuccessful attempt to provide a level surface and undistorted copies). TEN-SECOND BUSINESS FORMS features a durable comb binding that allows the book to lie absolutely flat on the copier. The result? Crisp, straight copies without effort, frustration or wear-and-tear.

TEN-SECOND BUSINESS FORMS is divided into 14 sections, each packed with valuable forms that will contribute to the profitability of your business in a different way:

CHAPTER 1. **ATTRACTING CUSTOMERS**
By using the professional forms provided in this chapter for

quotes, estimates, bids and proposals, you will increase your ability to attract customers. A professional-looking quote implies professional quality workmanship!

CHAPTER 2. **SALES CLOSERS**

By using the order forms, work orders and receipts in this chapter you will improve your ability to close sales, improve the accuracy of order-taking and help avoid problems with customers.

CHAPTER 3. **CUSTOMER CORRESPONDENCE**

By using the memos, packing slips and other forms in this chapter you will present a professional image to customers, bolstering their confidence in doing business with you.

CHAPTER 4. **SALES BUILDERS**

By keeping careful records and by following up every potential customer who phones your business or walks into your store, you can greatly increase your sales without buying expensive advertising. For salespeople, this chapter includes several call report forms as well as a client/prospect contact summary for carefully tracking calls to individual accounts: a powerful sales tool.

CHAPTER 5. **EXPENSE CONTROLLERS**

This chapter explains how you can reduce your expenses by carefully recording and evaluating your expenses on the forms provided. The forms in this chapter will also help you prepare your income tax returns and verify expenses that the IRS often challenges, such as telephone, auto, travel and meal expenses.

CHAPTER 6. **INVENTORY MANAGERS**

Careful inventory tracking can save a lot of time and money. This chapter provides forms just for this purpose as well as more specialized forms such as the out of stock notice, an important form for informing customers as to expected shipping dates of out of stock merchandise.

CHAPTER 7. CASH FLOW MAXIMIZERS

Professional-looking invoices and statements are essential to help insure that your bills get paid and that they get paid on time. Other forms in this chapter include invoice records, bank deposit forms and several forms for tracking cash.

CHAPTER 8. BAD DEBT COLLECTORS

The forms in this chapter will collect overdue bills efficiently and professionally. They will also help you decide which customers to extend credit to, when to cancel or limit credit, and how to track the payment of invoices by account.

CHAPTER 9. TIME PLANNERS

By using the time-planning forms in this chapter, you and your staff will get more work done in less time. You will be able to prioritize to avoid crises and to focus on the work that is most profitable.

CHAPTER 10. TIME SAVERS

The use of office memos, phone memos and other forms in this chapter will save time, insure that important phone calls are not missed, and add a touch of professionalism to office communication.

CHAPTER 11. PERSONNEL RECORDS

Even if you employ one part-time person you are required by law to keep detailed employment records.

CHAPTER 12. RESULT TRACKERS

Profit and loss statements and balance sheets are basic tools for managing a business and for obtaining bank loans and credit from suppliers.

CHAPTER 13. **BUSINESS GROWERS**

To grow your business you must plan carefully, giving close consideration to cash flow needs by projecting cash inflow and outflow and future balance sheets. This section also includes a form for projecting expenses for a new business.

CHAPTER 14. **BLANK GRIDS & CHARTS**

This chapter offers you dozens of blank grids and charts to create your own professional-looking business forms.

TEN-SECOND BUSINESS FORMS is packed with the widest array of business forms available, organized and explained to maximize your ability to profit from each and every one. But remember, by using just one form in this book, you will save a printing bill larger than the cost of the entire book. And if you are able to land just one more customer from a more professional presentation, or are able to collect just one more overdue bill, then you will pay for the cost of this book many times over.

Furthermore, remember that one of the most common reasons for small business failure is poor record keeping. TEN-SECOND BUSINESS FORMS makes record keeping both easy and profitable!

CHAPTER 1

Attracting Customers:

Forms for quotes, estimates, bids, and proposals

Whether your business is a one-person house painting service or a major engineering firm, your first meeting with a prospective customer is very important. Professional-looking forms such as the ones we have included in this chapter for *quotes, estimates, bids,* and *proposals,* go a long way towards projecting a professional image. A clean, well-organized quote implies professional, quality workmanship. It also implies that you are serious about your business, that you will fulfill your obligations, and that you can be counted on to complete the work on time.

Remember that once you have left the customer, all you leave behind is the form outlining your quote. When the prospective customer sits down to evaluate your quote, and those of your competitors, you can be assured that the professionally prepared quotes will have a competitive edge over ones scribbled on a piece of scrap paper, or the back of an envelope.

Simply put, professional-looking forms for quotes and estimates build customer confidence and will help turn prospects into customers.

QUOTATION

Date prepared   /   /

Valid until   /   /

Quotation number: _____

Prepared for:

Item/Description	Number Units	Unit price	Amount

Terms and conditions:

TOTAL

Prepared by: _____

QUOTATION

Date prepared   /   /

Valid until   /   /

Quotation number: _____

Prepared for:

Item/Description	Number Units	Unit price	Amount

Terms and conditions:

TOTAL

Prepared by: _____

QUOTATION

Date prepared   /   /

Valid until   /   /

Quotation number: _____

Prepared for:

Item/Description	Number Units	Unit price	Amount

Terms and conditions:

TOTAL

Prepared by: _____

ESTIMATE

Date   /   /

Item/Description

_____

_____

_____

_____

MATERIALS

Item/Description	Number	Cost per	Amount

MATERIAL COSTS [   ]

LABOR

Item/Description	Hours	Rate	Amount

LABOR COSTS [   ]

TOTAL
ESTIMATED
COSTS [   ]

BID

Date   /   /

Submitted by: _____

_____

For: _____

_____

Cost details:

Item/description	Amount

Total Bid Price

This price valid until: _____

Comments/Specifications

PROPOSAL

Date   /   /

Submitted for: _____   Submitted by: _____

_____   _____

_____   _____

SPECIFICATIONS: _____

_____

_____

_____

_____

_____

_____

_____

_____

_____

_____

_____

_____

_____

SCHEDULE: _____

COST: _____

TERMS: _____

CHAPTER 2

Sales Closers:

Order forms, work orders, receipts, and more

Neat, clean and well-organized *order forms* and *work orders* insure that your customers get the exact products and services that they want, when they want them. Professional order forms, properly prepared and processed, will also help avoid time-consuming and irritating follow-up phone calls to obtain more information. In addition, having an order form ready to be filled in can help close sales -- just as estimating a price or suggesting a product can often persuade a hesitant prospect to go ahead with the purchase.

Order forms can also improve relations with customers and avoid uncertainties or disputes. If a customer orders five items but later only remembers ordering four, and if you can produce the order form showing the actual order placed, a difficult situation can be avoided.

Additionally, by giving the customer a copy of a professional-looking order form, you will appear more professional and be treated more professionally. A customer will have more confidence in your product or service, even before the product is delivered or before the work begins.

Receipts are particularly important in a cash business. By keeping copies of each receipt, and giving a receipt to every customer, a business owner can double-check the cash position and ascertain that no cash has disappeared unaccounted for. To ensure that customers ask for a receipt, many businesses post signs at the check-out point saying: "No returns or refunds without a receipt."

Receipts are important in non-cash businesses as well. As with order forms, professional-looking receipts help build customers' confidence and underscore the fact that they are dealing with a professionally-run business.

WORK ORDER

Date / /

Item/Description
_____

_____

_____

_____

MATERIALS

Item/Description	Number	Cost per	Amount

MATERIAL COSTS [   ]

LABOR

Item/Description	Hours	Rate	Amount

LABOR COSTS [   ]

TOTAL
ESTIMATED
COSTS [   ]

PHONE ORDER

Number: _____

Account Number: _____

Shipping instructions: _____

Sold to: Ship to:

Number Ordered	Item/Description	Number Shipped	Number Backordered	Price Per	Extended

Terms: _____

Salesperson: _____

Date: / /

SUB TOTAL _____

SHIPPING _____

TOTAL

PHONE ORDER

Order date: /   /

Number: _____

Account number: _____

Shipping instructions: _____

Sold to:
                                         Ship to:

Customer

City: City:

State: Zip: State: Zip:

Attn: Attn:

Delivery date: /   /

Shipping date: /   /

Ship Via: _____

Quantity ordered	Item/Description	Number shipped	Per unit	Extended

TERMS OF PAYMENT

     Cash

     COD

     On account # _____

     Charge _____

     Other _____

SUBTOTAL _____

TOTAL

Salesperson: _____

Date: /   /

PHONE ORDER

Number: _____

Account Number: _____

Shipping instructions: _____

Sold to: Ship to:

Number Ordered	Item/Description	Number Shipped	Number Backordered	Price per	Extended

Terms: _____

Salesperson: _____

Date: ____ / ____ / ____

SUBTOTAL _____

SHIPPING _____

TOTAL

PHONE ORDER

Number: _____

Account Number: _____

Shipping instructions: _____

Sold to: Ship to:

Number Ordered	Item/Description	Number Shipped	Number Backordered	Price per	Extended

Terms: _____

Salesperson: _____

Date: ____ / ____ / ____

SUBTOTAL _____

SHIPPING _____

TOTAL

ORDER BLANK

Number: _____

Date: ___ / ___ / ___

Salesperson: _____

Sold to:

Ship to:

Telephone: ___ / ___ - ___

Ship by: _____

Date: ___ / ___ / ___

Quantity	Item/Description	Price per	Extended

TERMS OF PAYMENT:
Cash

On account # _____

COD

Charge _____

Other _____

SALES TAX _____

TOTAL _____

SHIPPING
CHARGE _____

**AMOUNT
DUE**

ORDER BLANK

Number: _____

Date: ____ / ____ / ____

Representative: _____

Sold to:

Ship to:

Telephone: ____ / ____ - ____

Ship by: ____ / ____ / ____

Date:

Quantity	Item/Description	Price per	Extended

TERMS OF PAYMENT:

Cash _____
COD _____
On account _____
Charge: _____
Other _____

SALES TAX _____

TOTAL _____

SHIPPING CHARGE _____

AMOUNT DUE [____]

ORDER BLANK

Number: _____

Date: ____ / ____ / ____

Representative: _____

Sold to:

Ship to:

Telephone: ____ / ____ - ____

Ship by: ____ / ____ / ____

Date:

Quantity	Item/Description	Price per	Extended

TERMS OF PAYMENT:

Cash _____
COD _____
On account _____
Charge: _____
Other _____

SALES TAX _____

TOTAL _____

SHIPPING CHARGE _____

AMOUNT DUE [____]

SPECIAL REQUEST

Number: _____

Date: __/__/__

Date required: __/__/__

Sold to:

City: Telephone: _____/_____

State: Zip:

Method of payment: Cash   Charge: _____   COD   Other: _____

Quantity	Item/Description	Unit Price	Extended

Salesperson: _____   **AMOUNT DUE**

SPECIAL REQUEST

Number: _____

Date: ___ / ___ / ___

Date required: ___ / ___ / ___

Sold to:

Telephone: ___ / ___ / ___ - ___

City:

State:

Zip:

Method of payment: Cash _____ Charge: _____ COD _____ Other: _____

Quantity	Item/Description	Unit Price	Extended

Salesperson: _____

BALANCE DUE

SPECIAL REQUEST

Number: _____

Date: ___ / ___ / ___

Date required: ___ / ___ / ___

Sold to:

Telephone: ___ / ___ / ___ - ___

City:

State:

Zip:

Method of payment: Cash _____ Charge: _____ COD _____ Other: _____

Quantity	Item/Description	Unit Price	Extended

Salesperson: _____

BALANCE DUE

SALES RECEIPT

Date: ___ / ___ / ___

Salesperson: _____

Name:

Street:

City:
State:
Zip:

Telephone: ___ / ___ - ___

Sold by   Cash   Charge: ___   COD   Other ___

Quantity	Item/Description	Price per	Extended

TOTAL

AMOUNT DUE

ALL RETURNS AND EXCHANGES MUST BE ACCOMPANIED BY THIS SLIP

SALES RECEIPT

Date: ___ / ___ / ___

Salesperson: _____

Name:

Street:

City:
State:
Zip:

Telephone: ___ / ___ - ___

Sold by   Cash   Charge: ___   COD   Other ___

Quantity	Item/Description	Price per	Extended

TOTAL

AMOUNT DUE

ALL RETURNS AND EXCHANGES MUST BE ACCOMPANIED BY THIS SLIP

RECEIPT

Date   /   /

Received from: _____

Amount: _____

Signed: _____

Receipt No. _____

TOTAL DUE	

This payment

BALANCE DUE

RECEIPT

Date   /   /

Received from: _____

Amount: _____

Signed: _____

Receipt No. _____

TOTAL DUE

This payment

BALANCE DUE

RECEIPT

Date   /   /

Received from: _____

Amount: _____

Signed: _____

Receipt No. _____

TOTAL DUE

This payment

BALANCE DUE

RECEIPT

Date   /   /

Received from: _____

Amount: _____

Signed: _____

Receipt No. _____

TOTAL DUE

This payment

BALANCE DUE

LAYAWAY RECORD

Date   /   /

Salesperson: _____

Sold to:

Telephone   /   -

Item/Description	Price per	Quantity	Extended

TOTAL _____

TAX _____

TOTAL DUE _____

DEPOSIT _____

BALANCE [   ]

Pick-up date   /   /

Delivery schedule:

LAYAWAY RECORD

Date   /   /

Salesperson: _____

Sold to:

Telephone   /   -

Item/Description	Price per	Quantity	Extended

TOTAL _____

TAX _____

TOTAL DUE _____

DEPOSIT _____

BALANCE [   ]

Pick-up date   /   /

Delivery schedule:

CHAPTER 3

Customer Correspondence:
Forms that professionalize your image

Any time you communicate with a customer, you need to maintain a professional image. For jotting a quick note to a customer, the *memo* form is perfect. By using this form you will present a professional image without going to the time of typing up a formal letter with complete address and greeting on letterhead. Because of its informal yet professional appearance, a memo allows you to zero-in on the issue at hand and skip formalities.

Packing slips are important to show the exact quantity and nature of the products you delivered. By using packing slips, you place the burden on the customer to challenge the accuracy of your delivery at the time of receipt. Otherwise, a business has no exact proof of the items and quantities shipped. Packing Slips also bring shipping errors to the surface quickly and allow you to resolve them before they become catastrophic problems.

Some companies have every packing slip initialed by the employee that picks and packs the shipment. This not only allows the firms to immediately identify the person who inaccurately picks or packs a shipment but, perhaps more importantly, also encourages shipping room personnel to take extra care in their work.

Packing slips are essential when you do business with any other company, even if you are selling only a single product. Without packing slips, you will probably need to wait longer to have your invoices processed -- and will occassionally be told that your shipment was never received.

Your business might use the *credit/debit memos* or *return authorization notices* only occasionally. However, the times that you have to use these forms (for example, when a bill is being disputed), might be a critical moment with an important customer -- a time when a professional-looking form, resolving the problem with the issuance of credit or debit, could make a difference in keeping the customer.

The *"We Missed You"* form is important, as well; it shows that you did your job and attempted to deliver your service or product on time, but that the customer was not there.

You can bolster your image by presenting yourself professionally every time you correspond with a customer. Since these forms frequently take even less time to write than a quick note, there is no reason not to appear professional in your correspondence!

MEMO

FROM _____   DATE   /   /

TO _____

SUBJECT _____

☐ URGENT

☐ FOR YOUR INFORMATION

☐ RESPOND

☐ PLEASE COMMENT

☐ OTHER _____

_____

_____

_____

_____

_____

_____

_____

_____

_____

_____

_____

_____

_____

_____

_____

_____

_____

PACKING SLIP

Date ___ / ___ / ___

Order number: _____

Invoice number: _____

Sold to: Ship to:

Number ordered	Item/Description	Number Shipped	Cartons	Total weight

TOTAL SHIPPED | | |

Packer: _____

PACKING SLIP

Number: _____

Date: ___ / ___ / ___

Salesperson: _____

Shipping
instructions: _____

Telephone: ___ / ___ - ___

Name:

Address:

City:
State:
Zip:

No. ordered	Item/Description	Shipped	Price per	Extended

SUBTOTAL _____

TOTAL

Received in good condition by: _____

PACKING SLIP

Number: _____

Date: ___ / ___ / ___

Salesperson: _____

Shipping
instructions: _____

Telephone: ___ / ___ - ___

Name:

Address:

City:
State:
Zip:

No. ordered	Item/Description	Shipped	Price per	Extended

SUBTOTAL _____

TOTAL

Received in good condition by: _____

PACKING SLIP

Date   /   /

Order number: _____

Invoice number: _____

Sold to: Ship to:

Number ordered	Item/Description	Number Shipped	Cartons	Total weight

Packer: _____   **TOTAL SHIPPED**

PACKING SLIP

Date   /   /

Order number: _____

Invoice number: _____

Sold to: Ship to:

Number ordered	Item/Description	Number Shipped	Cartons	Total weight

Packer: _____   **TOTAL SHIPPED**

CREDIT NOTICE

Date   /   /

Date issued: /   /

Customer Number: _____

Order Number: _____

Credit to:

Shipping address:

Dear Customer: We have adjusted your account to reflect the following transaction(s).

ITEMS RETURNED   Date received: /   /

Quantity	Item/Description	Price per	Extended	Explanation

TOTAL CREDIT ADJUSTMENT

Remarks:

_____

_____

_____

_____

Approved by: _____

Date   /   /

CREDIT NOTICE

Date / /

Customer number:
Order number: _____

Date issued: / /

To:

Shipping address: / /

Dear Customer: We have adjusted your account
to reflect the following transaction
GOODS RETURNED   Date received: / /

Quantity	Item/Description	Price per	Extended	Explanation

TOTAL CREDIT ADJUSTMENT

Remarks: _____

Approved by: _____

Date: / /

CREDIT NOTICE

Date / /

Customer number:
Order number: _____

Date issued: / /

To:

Shipping address: / /

Dear Customer: We have adjusted your account
to reflect the following transaction
GOODS RETURNED   Date received: / /

Quantity	Item/Description	Price per	Extended	Explanation

TOTAL CREDIT ADJUSTMENT

Remarks: _____

Approved by: _____

Date: / /

DEBIT NOTICE

Date   / - /

Date issued: /   /

Customer Number: _____

Order Number: _____

Credit to: Shipping address:

Dear Customer: We have adjusted your account to reflect the following transaction(s).

Quantity	Item/Description	Price per	Extended	Explanation

TOTAL DEBIT ADJUSTMENT

Remarks:

_____

_____

_____

_____

Approved by: _____

Date   /   /

DEBIT NOTICE

To:

Date _____ / _____ / _____

Customer number: _____

Order number: _____

Date issued: _____ / _____ / _____

Shipping address:

Dear Customer: We have adjusted your account to reflect the following transaction(s).

Quantity	Item/Description	Price per	Extended	Explanation

TOTAL DEBIT ADJUSTMENT

Remarks: _____

Approved by: _____

Date: _____ / _____ / _____

DEBIT NOTICE

To:

Date _____ / _____ / _____

Customer number: _____

Order number: _____

Date issued: _____ / _____ / _____

Shipping address:

Dear Customer: We have adjusted your account to reflect the following transaction(s).

Quantity	Item/Description	Price per	Extended	Explanation

TOTAL DEBIT ADJUSTMENT

Remarks: _____

Approved by: _____

Date: _____ / _____ / _____

AUTHORIZATION FOR RETURN

Date   /   /

Sold to: Return to:

Attn:

Order no: _____

Order date: /   /

Quantity	Item/Description	Unit price	Extended

TOTAL

Reason for return

Date   /   /

Approved by:

WE MISSED YOU

Name:

Address:

We were here on ___ / ___ / ___ at ___

Please call us at ___ - ___

between ___ and ___ to arrange another visit.

Signed: ___

WE MISSED YOU

Name:

Address:

We were here on ___ / ___ / ___ at ___

Please call us at ___ - ___

between ___ and ___ to arrange another visit.

Signed: ___

WE MISSED YOU

Name:

Address:

We were here on ___ / ___ / ___ at ___

Please call us at ___ - ___

between ___ and ___ to arrange another visit.

Signed: ___

WE MISSED YOU

Name:

Address:

We were here on ___ / ___ / ___ at ___

Please call us at ___ - ___

between ___ and ___ to arrange another visit.

Signed: ___

REQUEST FOR SAMPLES

Date: /   /

Name: _____   Title: _____   Address: _____

Company: _____   Telephone: _____   _____

_____

Previous Customer   New Account

Acct # _____   Acct # _____

_____

Quantity	Item/Description

TOTAL
QUANTITY

Shipping instructions: _____

Authorizing Signature: _____

CHAPTER 4

Sales Builders:

Forms that help increase your sales

Whether you have a hundred-person sales force or handle all of your customers personally, meticulous use of the enclosed forms can send your sales soaring!

Every person or business who shows an interest in your product or service is a qualified lead. Every person who calls your business asking for a quote -- or merely for information -- is a qualified lead. Every person who wanders into your shop is a qualified lead. Any one of these people is much more likely to buy your product or service than someone you have not had contact with. By carefully following up each precious qualified lead, you can greatly increase your customer base without spending any money for expensive advertising.

To follow up qualified leads, you need to ask prospective customers for their names and phone numbers or addresses. When a prospect calls to inquire about your service, try to first ask for their name and their phone number.

You can use the *sales lead tracking sheet* to take information from a prospective customer who inquires about your services or products over the phone. You can then follow-up by calling back the prospect in a few days to renew interest in your services or products. The sales lead tracking sheet is designed to allow you to make notes on several additional calls to a prospect. By using this sheet, you can keep track of when you last spoke with the prospect and what their level of interest and concerns were on the most recent call.

If you have a retail location, you can build up a large pool of qualified leads by simply putting the *mailing list* in a highly visible location with a small sign beside it. You can send simple mailings, such as postcards, to people on this list, reminding them of your services or products. A stronger inducement would be to announce a sale or, better yet, to send a coupon for a discount on their next purchase.

Of course, one of the strongest uses of the mailing list form is to build repeat sales within your existing customer base. If your product is one that the same customer can use more than once, then you should send mailings frequently. It is much easier to sell the same customer again than to attract a new customer. Even if your business is one which deals primarily with one-shot sales, such as an aluminum siding contracting business, you still can benefit tremendously by careful use of a mailing list. For example, you can ask existing customers to refer their friends and relatives to you and announce a special limited-time offer.

Every salesperson needs to keep careful records of his and her phone calls and customer visits; we have included several forms for this purpose. In addition, self-employed and other small businesspeople can benefit by carefully building lists of qualified prospects and by aggressively following up on them.

For salespeople and sales managers, detailed records are vital. *Sales reports* show the amount of completed contacts from one day to the next. Sales reports show who is worthwhile to follow up, who is not, when a prospect should be followed up, and what their primary needs or concerns are.

We offer a large variety of sales reports so that you can choose the one best suited to your own purposes. Included are a *daily appointment log*, a *telephone call report*, a *daily call report*, a *salesperson's visit log*, and a *salesperson's daily record*.

Sales reports are actually more effective for sales managers in evaluating the potential of salespeople than they are for sales reps. Sales reps are best served by having all of their information organized on an account-by-account, as opposed to a day-by-day, basis. A salesperson should have one centralized record of every previous conversation with an account in front of him or her when an account is called.

Again, we have included several forms to choose from: the *contact summary*, the *sales lead tracking sheet*, and the *proposal follow-up* all have room to summarize information from multiple contacts with a customer. A well-organized sales rep should rely primarily on these forms for keeping notes about prospects and customers, and should only use daily call reports and related forms to submit to sales managers. As soon as the sales rep feels it would be worthwhile to call a prospect a second time, he or she should start using a form such as the contact summary form. This way all of the information on the client will be on one form without the sales rep needing to take extra time to copy it from other forms, such as the daily call report.

Any small business owner or salesperson can increase their sales and earnings significantly by taking a small amount of time to maintain meticulous records on every qualified prospect and customer.

SALES LEAD TRACKING SHEET

Name: _____ Telephone: ___ / ___ - ___

Address: _____

Contact person: _____

Product: _____

Date	Contents of call	Follow-up	Remarks

SALES LEAD TRACKING SHEET

Name: _____ Telephone: ___ / ___ - ___

Address: _____

Contact person: _____

Product: _____

Date	Contents of call	Follow-up	Remarks

MAILING LIST

Page number   of

Date revised   /   /

Name	Address	Zip code	Customer #	Date added	Mailing sent	Delete

ADDRESS LIST

Page number   of

Date revised   /   /

Name	Address	Zip code	Area code	Telephone

DAILY APPOINTMENT LOG

Date   /   /

Client/Account	Service Type	Scheduled Visit	Begin Time	End Time	Next Visit Date	Comments

Name: _____

Location: _____

TELEPHONE CALL REPORT

Date from: /   /

Date to: /   /

Page   of

Name: Address:

Firm name/Location	Contact name/Title	Telephone Number	Result	$ Sold

Comments:

TOTAL SALES

DAILY CALL REPORT

Date: ___ / ___ / ___

Page ___ of ___

Name: _____

Product line: _____ Territory: _____

Address: _____

_____

Firm name/Location	Contact name/Title Telephone number	Result	Follow-up?	$ Sold

Comments:

TOTAL SALES

SALESPERSON'S VISIT LOG

Date: /   /

Page   of

Name: _____

_____

_____

Address: _____

_____

_____

Company name/Location	Contact name/Title	Telephone Number	Result	$ Sold	Follow-up?

Comments:

TOTAL SALES

SALESPERSON'S DAILY RECORD

SALESPERSON _____   DATE ___ / ___ / ___

Company Name	Address/ Telephone	Contact	Sold?	Comments

PAGE TOTALS: Contacts Made [   ]   Total Sales [   ]

CLIENT/PROSPECT CONTACT SUMMARY

Company: _____   Representative: _____

Contact: _____   Product: _____

Phone: ____ / ____ - ____

Address: _____

_____

Date	Comment	When to call next?	Sale?

PROPOSAL FOLLOW-UP

Date / /

Period from / / to / /

Representative: _____

	Date last contacted	Proposal	Response	Follow-up
Company:				
Address:				
Telephone: / -				
Contact:				
Company:				
Address:				
Telephone: / -				
Contact:				
Company:				
Address:				
Telephone: / -				
Contact:				
Company:				
Address:				
Telephone: / -				
Contact:				

DISCOUNT WORKSHEET

Date   /   /

Prepared by: _____

Item/Description	Retail price	Date valid from	Date valid to	Percent discount	Final unit price

CHAPTER 5

Expense Controllers:
Forms that control and reduce costs

If only for basic tax purposes, every business must be able to show expense totals by category. And if your business is ever audited, the IRS or State Tax Examiner will expect you to be able to show instantly how you derived the total for any expense category. As far as the tax auditors are concerned, if you can't immediately document an expenditure then the expenditure never occurred.

For example, when one of my businesses was audited, the examiner, who knew nothing about my business, said that my phone expenses seemed excessive and that I would have to immediately provide him with a summary of all the phone bills that I had paid. Fortunately, I had a neat summary of all of my expenses by category prepared on a form similar to the *expense record form*. Next, the auditor demanded two specific original phone invoices (you absolutely must save every single invoice you pay). As if that weren't enough, he insisted that my business phone calls were personal calls! If I had maintained a *telephone log report* I would have had nothing to worry about; since I didn't, he disallowed some of my business phone calls as personal calls. I was completely at his mercy without a phone call record; he could conceivably have disallowed deduction of my entire phone bill!

For income tax purposes, you must record each expense by category, as soon as the expense is made, on a form such as the *expense record*. Then, at year-end, before filling out your income tax forms, you must summarize your expenses by category using a form such as the *profit and loss statement*. You will want to record phone calls on a telephone logreport to show that they were business calls. Another area in which the IRS is particularly stringent is the deduction of car and truck expenses. The best procedure is to keep a complete daily log such as the *monthly expense report* showing exactly when you used a vehicle for business or pleasure.

Besides tax purposes, recording expenses is very important in managing your business. To control and reduce your expenses you must start by carefully logging and summarizing them by category -- as in the profit and loss statement and the expense record. Then look for areas where you can cut costs. Remember, any time you can cut expenses without cutting sales you are adding directly to your profits. If you have a 10% profit margin, then a 10% reduction in costs would add as much profit as a 100% increase in sales!

When you look at your expense record and try to reduce future costs, think not only of which expenses you might be able to avoid in the future, but also which purchases you might be able to find at a less expensive source of supply. The *request for bid* form will expedite obtaining estimates from several different suppliers. In fact, you will often get better terms from your existing suppliers by sending them a formal request for bid form before sending out a *purchase order* to complete the sale.

The use of a formal purchase order can be very important. Any company -- no matter how small -- that uses purchase orders is more likely to be extended credit than a firm that does not. Purchase orders are also important for other reasons. Written purchase orders give you complete control, without argument, over all specifications of products and services that you are buying. Without using written purchase orders, suppliers will frequently make minor substitutions or alterations in their products or deliveries that will make you unhappy. I have found this out the hard way -- you don't have to.

Purchase orders allow you to shave expenses, too. For example, by specifying the shipment method you may save money. Many suppliers consider a 10% or 15% overrun on a custom-made product (such as packing cartons) to be perfectly acceptable. If you do not want to accept an overrun, say so on the Purchase Order.

The *purchase order record* is crucial because it helps you to project your future cash needs. If you find that you are spending more than you can afford to, then hold off buying more goods -- or ask your suppliers for extended payment terms.

The *remittance form* is more important than you might think. You can save time by paying several bills from one supplier at one time (remememeber, time is money). Firms often incorrectly process payments; if you do not carefully identify which invoices you are paying, you can easily burn up many hours in discussions with accounts receivable departments. The use of the remittance form can help avoid confusion by showing a supplier exactly which bills you are paying at one time.

Salespeople often seem to expect larger paychecks than they earn. One reason is that they tend to forget about tax withholdings. In any event, you can reduce the chance of disagreement with a salesperson over commissions by using a well-organized form such as the *commission summary* or the *salesperson's summary*.

Remember, time spent carefully recording expenses will not only save hours later, but can also help reduce tax bills and help you decide in which areas of your business you can trim expenses.

EXPENSE RECORD

DATE	Amount of Expense	BUDGET CATEGORY												

TELEPHONE LOG REPORT

Date	Time	Caller	Department	Call to	Company/ address	City	Area code	Telephone number

PROFIT & LOSS STATEMENT

Year: _____

INCOME

Gross sales: _____

Less returns: _____

Less bad debt: _____

Interest, rent, royalty income: _____

TOTAL INCOME

EXPENSES

Cost of goods sold: _____

Direct payroll: _____

Indirect payroll: _____

Taxes, other than income tax: _____

Sales expenses: _____

Shipping, postage: _____

Advertising, promotion: _____

Office expenses: _____

Travel, entertainment: _____

Phone: _____

Other utilities: _____

Auto/truck: _____

Insurance: _____

Professional fees: _____

Rent: _____

Interest on loans: _____

Other: _____

TOTAL EXPENSES BEFORE TAX

NET INCOME

INCOME TAX _____

NET INCOME AFTER TAX

MONTHLY EXPENSE REPORT

For month of _____ 19___

Name _____

Day	Auto Mileage	Parking, tolls	Other transportation	Meals	Lodging	Other (describe)	Other ($ amount)	TOTAL
1								
2								
3								
4								
5								
6								
7								
8								
9								
10								
11								
12								
13								
14								
15								
16								
17								
18								
19								
20								
21								
22								
23								
24								
25								
26								
27								
28								
29								
30								
31								

Total Mileage [____] X [____] Amount per mile

Subtotal [____]
Mileage costs [____]
TOTAL [____]

67

MONTHLY EXPENSE REPORT

FROM: /   /   TO   /   /

NAME _____   POSITION _____

DAY	TRAVEL	AUTO	MEALS	LODG.	ENTERT.	OTHER	DAILY TOTALS
1							
2							
3							
4							
5							
6							
7							
8							
9							
10							
11							
12							
13							
14							
15							
16							
17							
18							
19							
20							
21							
22							
23							
24							
25							
26							
27							
28							
29							
30							
31							

REQUEST FOR BID

Date   /   /

Valid until   /   /

Quantity	Item/Description	Price per	Extended

Delivery and shipping requirements:

TOTAL

Signed: _____

REQUEST FOR BID

Date   /   /

Valid until   /   /

Quantity	Item/Description	Price per	Extended

Delivery and shipping requirements:

TOTAL

Signed: _____

PURCHASE ORDER

Date   /   /

Order # _____

Our Purchase Order Number must appear on all invoices, cases, packing lists and correspondence.

To:

Date Wanted: /   /

Terms: _____

Ship via: _____

Quantity	Item/Description	Price	Amount

_____
Authorized Signature

TOTAL COST

PURCHASE ORDER

Date   /   /

Order # _____

Our Purchase Order Number must appear on all invoices, cases, packing lists and correspondence.

To:

Date Wanted: /   /

Terms: _____

Ship via: _____

Quantity	Item/Description	Price	Amount

Authorized Signature _____

PURCHASE ORDER

Date   /   /

Order # _____

Our Purchase Order Number must appear on all invoices, cases, packing lists and correspondence.

To:

Date Wanted: /   /

Terms: _____

Ship via: _____

Quantity	Item/Description	Price	Amount

Authorized Signature _____

PURCHASE ORDER RECORD

Date from ___ / ___ / ___

Date to ___ / ___ / ___

Page _____ of _____

P.O. Number	Date	Issued to	Item/Description	Due	Total Amount

SHEET TOTAL

REMITTANCE

Date: /   /

YOUR INVOICE #		
Invoice #	Date	Amount

DEDUCTIONS			
Date	Explanation	Amount	Discount

AMOUNT PAID

REMITTANCE

Date: /   /

YOUR INVOICE #		
Invoice #	Date	Amount

DEDUCTIONS			
Date	Explanation	Amount	Discount

AMOUNT PAID

VOUCHER/ACCOUNTS PAYABLE

Date / /

Voucher number: _____

Payable to:	Date	Account number	Extended
Approved by:			
Date / /			
Check number: _____			

TOTAL _____

NET PAYABLE

Comments:

VOUCHER/ACCOUNTS PAYABLE

Date / /

Voucher number: _____

Payable to:	Date	Account number	Extended
Approved by:			
Date / /			
Check number: _____			

TOTAL _____

NET PAYABLE

Comments:

COMMISSION SUMMARY

Period from: / /

Period to: / /

Salesperson Name: _____

Territory: _____

Date	Order number	Client	Extended	Commission percentage	Amount

TOTAL INVOICED

GROSS COMMISSION EARNED _____

LESS ADVANCE _____

OTHER DEDUCTIONS _____

Date paid: / /

AMOUNT PAYABLE

SALESPERSON'S SUMMARY

Date from: /   /

Date to: /   /

Name: _____

Date	Order #	Client	Extended	Commission Percentage	Amount

TOTAL INVOICED SALES

GROSS COMMISSION EARNED _____

LESS ADVANCES _____

Date Paid: /   /

COMMISSION DUE

SALESPERSON'S SUMMARY

Date from: /   /

Date to: /   /

Name: _____

Date	Order #	Client	Extended	Commission Percentage	Amount

TOTAL INVOICED SALES

GROSS COMMISSION EARNED _____

LESS ADVANCES _____

Date Paid: /   /

COMMISSION DUE

CHAPTER 6

Inventory Managers:
Forms that control your inventory

The importance of inventory management is often overlooked by small businesses. Nevertheless, it is impossible to manage your inventory too closely.

Many small businesspeople underestimate the cost of carrying inventory and the cost of stocking out. Too much inventory will bloat your costs, eat up your cash, and kill your growth prospects! But inventory stock-outs will not only kill potential sales, but can also lose customers permanently.

First, remember that the money you have invested in inventory costs you more than the interest on the inventory loan or the amount that this money could earn you in the bank. Why? The money you have tied up in inventory could be used to expand your business, where it could probably earn you a lot more money than in the bank! Then there is the cost of insuring the inventory, the cost of shipping it in, and inventory taxes. Another very important cost is the cost of storing the inventory. You say storage doesn't cost you anything because you don't rent a separate building for it? Think again. If you have a retail store and a storeroom at the same location, the storage cost might be the same as the additional revenue you could gain by enlarging your retail area into the storeroom area. Even if you do not have a retail store, storage space always has other uses such as accomodating a larger work area or a more efficient shipping room.

Another cost in carrying inventory is the risk of damage, and, more importantly, the risk of obsolescence. If your inventory is outdated by a newer version and you can't return it, you could take a major loss.

Of course, any time you are out of stock of an item you risk losing the sale. You can minimize this risk by using two forms. The first is the *out of stock notice*. By sending this form to a customer (or distributing it in the store) you can keep the customer's order and tell them when you will expect to receive the item. Another form that will help is the *backorder record.* Here you need to carefully record all orders for items that are out of stock. This way you can keep track of how many and which out of stock items you need and press suppliers accordingly. However, the more you stock out, the greater the risk of losing customers. (Our firm switched suppliers of office supplies primarily because the previous vendor stocked out so frequently.)

The *inventory report* is the basic form for controlling inventory. By keeping inventory records you will know exactly what is in stock and how fast it is selling (by looking at the previous inventory reports). Then you can project when you should reorder to minimize excess inventory on hand and also minimize the chance of stocking out. We have included several inventory report forms; one of the basic differences between them is that some allow you to trace all deliveries and shipments on an individual item, whereas others are designed for recording a physical count of many different items on one form.

Daily shipping records are useful because they allow you to tell inquiring customers when to expect their orders. They can also help substantiate claims that items were shipped by you. However, a signature that the goods were received is the only way to truly substantiate that goods were delivered, not just shipped.

Receiving slips are also important. They prevent you from having to rely on the packing slip from your vendor for accuracy. As soon as a shipment is received, you should fill out the receiving slip, checking the quantity and quality of the goods delivered.

If your business maintains an inventory, you will find it to be an area that constitutes one of your largest yearly costs. Use these forms rigorously to control and reduce your inventory expenses.

OUT OF STOCK NOTICE

Date   /   /

Order number: _____

Order date   /   /

We cannot fill your order at this time because the items listed are temporarily out of stock.
We apologize for the inconvenience.

Item/description	Quantity	Estimated shipping date

OUT OF STOCK NOTICE

Date   /   /

Order number: _____

Order date   /   /

We cannot fill your order at this time because the items listed are temporarily out of stock.
We apologize for the inconvenience.

Item/description	Quantity	Estimated shipping date

BACKORDER RECORD

Date from: /   /

Date to: /   /

Item/Description	Number Ordered	Number Back-ordered	Date ordered from supplier	Date due	Date received

BACKORDER RECORD

Date from: /   /
Date to: /   /

Item/Description	Number Ordered	Number Back-ordered	Date ordered from supplier	Date due	Date received

BACKORDER RECORD

Date from: /   /
Date to: /   /

Item/Description	Number Ordered	Number Back-ordered	Date ordered from supplier	Date due	Date received

INVENTORY REPORT

Date from   /   /

Date to   /   /

DATE	DESCRIPTION	RECEIVED				SHIPPED		NET STOCK
		P.O. #	Cost per	Amount	Receiver	Order #	Quantity	

INVENTORY REPORT

Date   /   /

Page number   of

Department: _____

Location: _____

	Quantity	Unit	Item/Description	Unit price	Extended	Total
1						
2						
3						
4						
5						
6						
7						
8						
9						
10						
11						
12						
13						
14						
15						
16						
17						
18						
19						
20						
21						
22						
23						
24						
25						

PREPARED BY:

TOTAL

INVENTORY REPORT

Date   /   /

Item/Description   _____

Location   _____

RECEIVED				RELEASED			NET
Date received	Purchase Order	Amount	Received	Date shipped	Invoice number	Amount	STOCK

INVENTORY REPORT

Date   /   /

Item/Description: _____

Location: _____

RECEIVED				SHIPPED			NET
Date received	Purchase number	Amount	Receiver	Date Shipped	Invoice number	Amount	STOCK

INVENTORY REPORT

Date   /   /

Item/Description: _____

Location: _____

RECEIVED				SHIPPED			NET
Date received	Purchase number	Amount	Receiver	Date Shipped	Invoice number	Amount	STOCK

INVENTORY CHANGES

Item/Description: _____

Sheet Number: _____

ORDERED

Date	Purchase Order #	Quantity	Due

RECEIVED

Date	Purchase Order #	Quantity

SOLD

Date	Invoice #	Amount sold	Net stock	Date	Invoice #	Amount sold	Net stock

DAILY SHIPPING RECORD

Date   /   /

Page   of

Customer	Invoice number	Item/Description	Shipping address	Carrier	Zone	Cartons	Weight	Shipper

RECEIVING SLIP

Date: /   /

Order/
Invoice No.:

Delivered to:

The following have been received in good order:

Quantity	Item/Description

Received by: _____

RECEIVING SLIP

Date: /   /

Order/
Invoice No.:

Delivered to:

The following have been received in good order:

Quantity	Item/Description

Received by: _____

MERCHANDISE RETURN

Date   /   /

From: _____   Address: _____

Telephone: /   -   _____

                                      _____

Quantity	Invoice/Order #	Item/Description	Price per	Extended

Credit as:

Exchange

Credit

Cash

Check # _____

Charge _____

TOTAL RETURN

Quantity   Amount

Reason for return:

MERCHANDISE EXCHANGE

Date   /   /

From: _____   Address: _____

Telephone: /   -   _____

                                            _____

Quantity	Invoice/Order #	Item/Description	Price per	Extended

TOTAL EXCHANGE

Quantity   Amount

Reason for exchange:

CHAPTER 7

Cash Flow Maximizers:

Professional invoices, statements and cash records

Simply by issuing professional-looking invoices and statements, a small business will have its bills paid sooner. In fact, it may very well avoid the collection problems caused by unprofessional-looking invoices. This is especially true when dealing with other businesspeople, but it is also true when billing consumers.

Because professional-looking invoices are critical for all businesses, we have included several different *invoice* forms from which to choose.

In one of my first businesses, I presented a client with an invoice I had produced quickly on a typewriter ten minutes before our scheduled meeting. His response: "What's this thing?" He may well have known it was an invoice, but he was definitely appalled at its unprofessional appearance. He did pay the bill -- but if I had mailed him the invoice instead of showing up for payment in person, I might not have been so lucky. Even if I had "only" had to wait an extra week or two for payment, the point still stands -- an invoice says a lot about the company that issues it, and about the likelihood of prompt payment.

Some businesses prefer to pay by *statements*, especially when you make more than one sale to them in a single month. Statements are sent in addition to, not instead of, invoices. By taking extra time to send statements in addition to invoices you can often speed payment and avoid follow-up phone calls.

Many businesses and consumers simply do not bother to pay their bills until they are reminded several times. In the following section on Bad Debt Collectors you'll find a variety of forms with which to collect old bills. However, the first step is to keep carefully organized records of money that is due to you on the *invoice record form.*

The best way to avoid billing problems and to speed cash flow is to get paid in advance. By using the *pro forma invoice* you can ask for payment in advance in a professional manner. This way, the customer has a copy of the invoice before he or she pays the bill, even though the service or goods have yet to be delivered.

The *bank deposit record* allows you to double-check payments from customers. If your customer insists that he or she paid a bill but you did not mark it as paid on your invoice record, you can double-check your bank deposit record. As your business grows, you will be surprised how often this situation will occur.

The other forms in this section help you control the flow of cash. If you are in a cash business, you must always be on your guard to track your cash trail as carefully as possible.

Remember, all firms and consumers expect professional-looking bills from any business, no matter how small. If you want to get paid and get paid on time for your service or products, be sure to use professional-looking invoices and statements.

Send payment to:

INVOICE
PLEASE PAY FROM THIS INVOICE; NO STATEMENT WILL BE ISSUED

Sold to: Ship to:

INVOICE NO.: _____

ACCOUNT NO.: _____

ORDER NO.: _____

SALESPERSON: _____

DATE: /   /

> Please indicate invoice number in all communications regarding this invoice.

No. ordered	No. shipped	Item/Description	Unit price	Amount

SALES TAX _____

SHIPPING/ HANDLING _____

AMOUNT DUE

THANK YOU FOR YOUR ORDER

Send payment to:

INVOICE

PLEASE PAY FROM THIS INVOICE;
NO STATEMENT WILL BE ISSUED

Sold to: Ship to:

INVOICE NO.: _____   SALESPERSON: _____

ORDER NO.: _____   DATE: /   /

ACCOUNT NO.: _____

Please indicate our invoice number in all
communications regarding this invoice.

No. ordered	No. shipped	Item/Description	Unit price	Amount

SALES TAX _____

SHIPPING/
HANDLING _____

THANK YOU FOR YOUR ORDER!

**AMOUNT
DUE**

Send payment to:

INVOICE

PLEASE PAY FROM THIS INVOICE;
NO STATEMENT WILL BE ISSUED

Sold to: Ship to:

INVOICE NO.: _____   SALESPERSON: _____

ORDER NO.: _____   DATE: /   /

ACCOUNT NO.: _____

Please indicate our invoice number in all
communications regarding this invoice.

No. ordered	No. shipped	Item/Description	Unit price	Amount

SALES TAX _____

SHIPPING/
HANDLING _____

THANK YOU FOR YOUR ORDER!

**AMOUNT
DUE**

Send payment to:

INVOICE

PLEASE PAY THIS INVOICE;
NO STATEMENT WILL BE SENT

INVOICE NO.: _____   DATE: /   /

Customer name: ORDER NO.: _____

Company: SALESPERSON: _____

Street: SHIPPED BY: _____

City:

State: Zip:

Quantity	Item/description	Price per	Amount

SHIPPING/HANDLING _____

THANK YOU FOR YOUR ORDER   **AMOUNT**
                                  DUE

Send payment to:

INVOICE

PLEASE PAY THIS INVOICE;
NO STATEMENT WILL BE SENT

INVOICE NO.: _____   DATE: /   /

Customer name: ORDER NO.: _____

Company: SALESPERSON: _____

Street: SHIPPED BY: _____

City:

State: Zip:

Quantity	Item/description	Price per	Amount

SHIPPING/HANDLING _____

THANK YOU FOR YOUR ORDER   **AMOUNT**
                                  DUE

Send payment to:

Sold to: Ship to:

INVOICE NO.: _____

ACCOUNT NO.: _____

ORDER NO.: _____

SALESPERSON: _____

DATE: /   /

Please indicate invoice and account number in all communications regarding this invoice.

No. ordered	Item/Description	Unit price	Amount

SALES TAX _____

SHIPPING/ HANDLING _____

AMOUNT DUE

INVOICE FOR WORK PERFORMED

Prepared by: _____

Date ___ / ___ / ___

MATERIALS

Date	Item/Description	Quantity	Unit price	Amount

TOTAL [ ]

LABOR

Date	Name/Department	Hours	Rate	Amount

TOTAL [ ]

TRAVEL AND MISCELLANEOUS EXPENSES

Date	Description	Amount

TOTAL [ ]

TOTAL INVOICE

Item	Amount
Materials:	
Labor:	
Travel/ Misc.	
Other	

TOTAL DUE [ ]

Account # _____

To:

STATEMENT

Date   /   /

_____

From: _____

_____

Date:	Invoice #	Item/Description	Amount
		Balance forward	
		Payment -- THANK YOU!	

PLEASE PAY
THIS AMOUNT

Account # _____

| STATEMENT |

To:

_____

Date   /   /

_____

From:

_____

Date:	Invoice #	Item/Description	Amount
		Balance forward	
		Payment -- THANK YOU!	

PLEASE PAY
THIS AMOUNT [   ]

Account # _____

| STATEMENT |

To:

_____

Date   /   /

_____

From:

_____

Date:	Invoice #	Item/Description	Amount
		Balance forward	
		Payment -- THANK YOU!	

PLEASE PAY
THIS AMOUNT [   ]

INVOICE RECORD

Month of:

Page number: ___ of ___ 19___

Invoice #	Invoice date	Invoice Amount	Company	Item/description	Date paid	Check number

BANK DEPOSIT RECORD

Date / /

Page of

CHECKS

	Name	$		
1				
2				
3				
4				
5				
6				
7				
8				
9				
10				
11				
12				
13				
14				
15				
16				
17				
18				

CHECKS

	Name	$		
19				
20				
21				
22				
23				
24				
25				
26				
27				
28				
29				
30				
31				
32				
33				
34				
35				
36				

TRAVELLER'S CHECKS

	Name	$		
1				
2				
3				
4				

CASH

	$	
CASH		

TOTAL CHECKS

TOTAL TRAVELLER'S CHECKS

CASH

TOTAL DEPOSIT

Account #

BANK DEPOSIT RECORD

Date   /   /

Page   of

CHECKS:		
	Name	$
1		
2		
3		
4		
5		
6		
7		
8		
9		
10		
11		
12		
13		
14		
15		
16		
17		
18		
19		
20		

TOTAL

TRAVELLER'S CHECKS:

TOTAL

CASH:

TOTAL

Remarks:

TOTAL CHECKS _____

TOTAL TRAVELLER'S CHECKS _____

CASH _____

TOTAL DEPOSIT

Account # _____

DAILY CASH RECORD

Date   /   /

Page   of

CASH RECEIVED FROM:	
Name	$
1	
2	
3	
4	
5	
6	
7	
8	
9	
10	
11	
12	
13	
14	
15	
16	
17	
18	
19	
20	

TOTAL RECEIPTS

CASH PAID OUT:	
Name	$
1	
2	
3	
4	
5	
6	
7	
8	
9	
10	

TOTAL

Remarks:

TOTAL RECEIPTS _____

LESS MONIES PAID OUT _____

BALANCE

PETTY CASH LEDGER

Date from   /   /

Date to   /   /

Prepared by: _____

Checked by: _____

Date	Payment Number	Cash to	Amount paid	Cash added	Balance
		BALANCE ON HAND			

TOTALS

PAID   ADDED

BALANCE FORWARDED

CASH DISBURSEMENT RECORD

Date from   /   /

Date to   /   /

Prepared by: _____

Checked by: _____

Date	Cash paid to	For item/description	Disbursed by	Account charged	Amount paid

CASHIER'S TILL RECORD

Name: _____

Date ___ / ___ / ___

Amount in till at
start of day _____

ITEM	BEGIN	END
Pennies		
Nickels		
Dimes		
Quarters		
Halves		
Dollars		
Fives		
Tens		
Twenties		
Fifties		
Hundreds		
Checks/Other		

TOTAL

Cashier Signature: _____

CASHIER'S TILL RECORD

Name: _____

Date ___ / ___ / ___

Amount in till at
start of day _____

ITEM	BEGIN	END
Pennies		
Nickels		
Dimes		
Quarters		
Halves		
Dollars		
Fives		
Tens		
Twenties		
Fifties		
Hundreds		
Checks/Other		

TOTAL

Cashier Signature: _____

CASHIER'S VOUCHER

Voucher # _____

Date ___ / ___ / ___

Item/Description: _____

Requested by: _____

Approved by: _____

Paid to:

Amount:

CASHIER'S VOUCHER

Voucher # _____

Date ___ / ___ / ___

Item/Description: _____

Requested by: _____

Approved by: _____

Paid to:

Amount:

CASHIER'S VOUCHER

Voucher # _____

Date ___ / ___ / ___

Item/Description: _____

Requested by: _____

Approved by: _____

Paid to:

Amount:

CASHIER'S VOUCHER

Voucher # _____

Date ___ / ___ / ___

Item/Description: _____

Requested by: _____

Approved by: _____

Paid to:

Amount:

VOUCHER/PETTY CASH

Date ___ / ___ / ___

Voucher # _____

Description of Use	Amount

TOTAL

Account # _____

Approved by: _____

VOUCHER/PETTY CASH

Date ___ / ___ / ___

Voucher # _____

Description of Use	Amount

TOTAL

Account # _____

Approved by: _____

VOUCHER/PETTY CASH

Date ___ / ___ / ___

Voucher # _____

Description of Use	Amount

TOTAL

Account # _____

Approved by: _____

VOUCHER/PETTY CASH

Date ___ / ___ / ___

Voucher # _____

Description of Use	Amount

TOTAL

Account # _____

Approved by: _____

CHAPTER 8

Bad Debt Collectors:

Forms that turn bad debts into cash

Some small businesses have bad debt running as high as 10% of sales, while other businesses keep it under 1%. By rigorously using the forms in this section you can keep your bad debt to an absolute minimum. Furthermore, you can use these forms to get your bills paid quickly and thereby increase the amount of cash you have on hand.

Most customers will eventually pay their bills. Some customers, as a matter of course, pay their bills extemely late -- and a few simply don't have enough money on hand to keep up with all their bills. You should avoid extending credit to these bad credit risks. To do this, simply have accounts apply for credit by filling out an *application for credit*, then take the time to check their references. If their credit is poor, insist that they pay in advance (use the pro forma invoice in the previous chapter). If their credit is questionable and you are unsure about extending credit, ask for partial payment and issue a receipt from the Sales Closers section of this book.

If you do decide to allow a customer to buy on credit, set up a credit limit and stick to it! Use the *credit record* to see that the customer is keeping current on their bills and that their total amount of credit is within your pre-assigned limit. Review each account regularly, and if an account is paying their bills more slowly than you would like, either cancel or reduce their credit line.

For all invoices and accounts that are overdue, you should promptly and regularly send out a *past due notice*. It is important to send these out at regular intervals to show the account that you are aware of the delay in payment and that you are serious about collecting it. Send out past due notices at least once a month.

Most overdue accounts will pay in full after receiving an overdue notice or two, but some always wait for a phone call. The *collection report* should be used to keep notes on calling overdue accounts. An alternative form to use is the contact summary form in the Sales Builders section of this book. Another alternative is to use the credit record form for recording overdue notices sent and overdue calls made. This form can also be used instead of the invoice record for recording sales to customers. Whichever forms you use, keep them in a safe place and keep them well-organized. Ideally, you should keep photocopies of all accounts receivable records in another location as well.

The *accounts receivable aging chart* is useful for showing the volume and age of your overdue accounts at the moment. It is also helpful in determining which overdue accounts to pursue first. In addition, this chart can help you project when you will be receiving payments from customers (for planning future cash flows as discussed later in the book).

Finally, the *returned check notification* form will make a strong impression on anyone who has written you a bad check. And if you haven't seen a bad check yet, you haven't been in business very long!

You have expended an enormous amount of time and money producing your goods and services, so be sure to go the extra distance to get paid for your work. Use these forms to collect every penny that you deserve!

APPLICATION FOR CREDIT

Date   /   /

Please complete all sections, including account numbers and income sources. Alimony, child support payments, and public aid need not be included if you do not wish them to be considered as supporting your application for credit.

Name: Telephone: / -	**Address:** City: State: Zip: Length of time at this address:
Previous address:	City: State: Zip:
Current employer: Period employed: Supervisor: Telephone: / - Position:	**Address:** City: State: Zip: Yearly salary:
Previous Employer: Period employed: Supervisor: Telephone: / - Position:	**Address:** City: State: Zip: Yearly salary:

Bank reference
(Account numbers):   Checking:
                        Savings:
                        Name of bank:
	Other income:

Other credit references: 1 _____
(Include daytime
telephone numbers):   2 _____

                        3 _____

CREDIT RECORD

Name:

Account no.:

Home address

Credit line   Date

_____   _____

Home telephone   /   -

Business address: _____   _____

_____   _____

Business telephone: /   -

Order number	Payment due		Payment received		Balance	First notice	2nd notice
	Amount	Date	Amount	Date			

1st overdue call:	
2nd overdue call:	
3rd overdue call:	

CREDIT RECORD

Name:
Account no.:
Home address:

Home telephone: /   -
Business address:

Business telephone: /   -

Credit line   Date

_____ _____

_____ _____

_____ _____

Order number	Payment due		Payment received		Balance	First notice	2nd notice
	Amount	Date	Amount	Date			

1st overdue call: _____

2nd overdue call: _____   3rd overdue call: _____

CREDIT RECORD

Name:
Account no.:
Home address:

Home telephone: /   -
Business address:

Business telephone: /   -

Credit line   Date

_____ _____

_____ _____

_____ _____

Order number	Payment due		Payment received		Balance	First notice	2nd notice
	Amount	Date	Amount	Date			

1st overdue call: _____

2nd overdue call: _____   3rd overdue call: _____

ACCOUNT RECORD

Account Number: _____

Account Name: _____

DATE	ITEM/DESCRIPTION	CHARGE	CREDIT	BALANCE
	Balance forward			

PAST DUE NOTICE

Date   /   /

Account no: _____

Your account is past due. Please remit the amount specified below.

Invoice Number	Item/description	Amount due	Payment due

AMOUNT DUE [   ]

PAST DUE NOTICE

Date   /   /

Account no: _____

Your account is past due. Please remit the amount specified below.

Invoice Number	Item/description	Amount due	Payment due

AMOUNT DUE

PAST DUE NOTICE

Date   /   /

Account no: _____

Your account is past due. Please remit the amount specified below.

Invoice Number	Item/description	Amount due	Payment due

AMOUNT DUE

COLLECTION REPORT

Company name: _____

Telephone number: _____

Address: _____

_____

_____

1. Date ___ / ___ / ___ Contact _____ Invoice # _____

   Results: Amount _____

2. Date ___ / ___ / ___ Contact _____ Invoice # _____

   Results: Amount _____

3. Date ___ / ___ / ___ Contact _____ Invoice # _____

   Results: Amount _____

4. Date ___ / ___ / ___ Contact _____ Invoice # _____

   Results: Amount _____

5. Date ___ / ___ / ___ Contact _____ Invoice # _____

   Results: Amount _____

6. Date ___ / ___ / ___ Contact _____ Invoice # _____

   Results: Amount _____

7. Date ___ / ___ / ___ Contact _____ Invoice # _____

   Results: Amount _____

ACCOUNTS RECEIVABLE AGING CHART

Date from   /   /

Date to   /   /

Customer	Invoice date	Invoice number	Item description	Current	30-60 days	60-90 days	90 days or more	Total
TOTAL								

RETURNED CHECK NOTIFICATION

Date: /   /

Telephone: /   -

Customer:

Address:

City:

State: Zip:

Your check no: _____

Amount: _____

Date of check: /   /

Bank: _____

We hold your check returned unpaid from your bank. Please send new payment immediately.

Signed: _____

RETURNED CHECK NOTIFICATION

Date: /   /

Telephone: /   -

Customer:

Address:

City:

State: Zip:

Your check no: _____

Amount: _____

Date of check: /   /

Bank: _____

We hold your check returned unpaid from your bank. Please send new payment immediately.

Signed: _____

CHAPTER 9

Time Planners:

Forms that turn time into money

In business, time is money! Every minute of every business day is time that could be spent making money. Unfortunately, some time must be spent in non-revenue-related tasks such as paying bills, paying taxes, cleaning the office, etcetera. Such tasks reduce the amount of time that can be spent on revenue-producing work making such time even more precious.

By using the *daily, weekly, monthly,* and *yearly organizers* you can prioritize your work, use your time more effectively, and make more money in less time. Before the end of every day, you should fill in the daily organizer for the following day. And before the end of each week, you should fill in the weekly organizer for the next week. The monthly and yearly organizers are less important for day-to-day affairs and you will refer to them primarily when making long-term plans. Under the "Urgent" column of the daily organizer, list the tasks that are most important and make sure that they get done. Then, if you get distracted with unforseen tasks and can't finish all of your plans for the day, at least you will have done the most important.

If you do not prioritize your tasks you will tend to give first priority to those tasks that come to mind first and that are the most time sensitive. Often these are not the most important tasks for increasing the profitability of your business.

Organizers are also important for listing appointments and events. By using your organizers for listing appointments, events and tasks, you will get into the habit of referring to them frequently and will increase your efficiency at work.

The *staffing calendar* will be quite valuable even if you have only two or three employees. By planning staff assignments on the same piece of paper, you can easily reassign work among different people. For example, by filling in the staffing calendar you might see that two employees are planning to do the same task -- allowing you to simply change assignments.

By using the staffing calendar and organizers, you will also be able to project more accurately when you will complete projects and when you will be able to start new ones: your customers will particularly appreciate this.

While all of the forms in this chapter are useful, The Daily Organizer is an extremely powerful personal management tool that creates more time in every working day. Once you start using the daily organizer you'll wonder how you ever got by without it!

DAILY ORGANIZER

Date: /   /

Time		URGENT
6:00		
:30		
7:00		
:30		
8:00		
:30		
9:00		
:30		
10:00		
:30		
11:00		
:30		
12:00		
:30		
1:00		
:30		
2:00		
:30		
3:00		
:30		
4:00		
:30		
5:00		
:30		
6:00		
:30		
7:00		
:30		
8:00		
:30		
9:00		

WEEKLY ORGANIZER

Week beginning: /   /

Ending: /   /

Time	Monday	Tuesday	Wednesday	Thursday	Friday	Saturday	Sunday
6:00							
:30							
7:00							
:30							
8:00							
:30							
9:00							
:30							
10:00							
:30							
11:00							
:30							
12:00							
:30							
1:00							
:30							
2:00							
:30							
3:00							
:30							
4:00							
:30							
5:00							
:30							
6:00							
:30							
7:00							
:30							
8:00							

MONTHLY ORGANIZER

Month of:

	Morning	Afternoon	Evening
1			
2			
3			
4			
5			
6			
7			
8			
9			
10			
11			
12			
13			
14			
15			
16			
17			
18			
19			
20			
21			
22			
23			
24			
25			
26			
27			
28			
29			
30			
31			

Comments:

YEARLY ORGANIZER

For year   19

	January	February	March	April	May	June
1						
2						
3						
4						
5						
6						
7						
8						
9						
10						
11						
12						
13						
14						
15						
16						
17						
18						
19						
20						
21						
22						
23						
24						
25						
26						
27						
28						
29						
30						
31						

YEARLY ORGANIZER

For year   19

	July	August	September	October	November	December
1						
2						
3						
4						
5						
6						
7						
8						
9						
10						
11						
12						
13						
14						
15						
16						
17						
18						
19						
20						
21						
22						
23						
24						
25						
26						
27						
28						
29						
30						
31						

STAFFING CALENDAR

Date from   /   /

Date to   /   /

Employee	Monday	Tuesday	Wednesday	Thursday	Friday	Saturday	Sunday

MEETING PLANNER

Date   /   /

Time	Subject	Persons Attending	Urgent
6-6:30			
6:30-7			
7-7:30			
7:30-8			
8-8:30			
8:30-9			
9-9:30			
9:30-10			
10-10:30			
10:30-11			
11-11:30			
11:30-12			
12-12:30			
12:30-1			
1-1:30			
1:30-2			
2-2:30			
2:30-3			
3-3:30			
3:30-4			
4-4:30			
4:30-5			
5-5:30			
5:30-6			
6-6:30			
6:30-7			
7-7:30			
7:30-8			
8-8:30			
8:30-9			

REMINDER

DATE: /   /

	THINGS TO DO	
1		
2		
3		
4		
5		
6		
7		
8		
9		
10		
	FOLLOW-UP	
1		
2		
3		

REMINDER

DATE: /   /

	THINGS TO DO	
1		
2		
3		
4		
5		
6		
7		
8		
9		
10		
	FOLLOW-UP	
1		
2		
3		

NOTES

Date   /   /

CHAPTER 10

Time-Savers:

Forms that speed office communication

It bears repeating -- time is money. The forms in this chapter are designed to make communication within a business as fast, simple and efficient as possible.

The basic *memo* and *phone memo* forms can save a lot of time. Instead of writing out a long note, an employee can jot down two names, one check mark, and three explanatory words to make a complete memo-type message. Why waste time with intricate office communication when you could be spending time on revenue-producing work with customers?

The *memo/response form* is a variation on the memo that will not only save you time in delivering a message but, more importantly, will also speed a reply by telling the person on the other end that they only need to jot down a few words in response -- not produce a detailed, elaborate reply.

The *routing label* can save time in two ways. The first is that the label takes about two seconds to fill out. More importantly, a routing label presents a clear instruction for the same item to pass from one person to the next. This avoids copying or reproducing the item or having to personally deliver it to every person on the list.

The *items needed form* can save more time than you might think. By having this form in a visible place, anyone can request (but not automatically receive) any supply they feel will improve their work. Having this form readily available means that the person responsible for ordering supplies does not have to be interrupted every time someone needs to order a special-colored pen. It also means that when you do need a supply ordered, you don't have to waste time looking for the person who orders supplies -- you can merely add it to the list.

In addition to saving time, forms such as these will add to your business a touch of professionalism which is an essential component of employee morale.

MEMO

FROM _____   DATE ___ / ___ / ___

TO _____

SUBJECT _____

☐ URGENT

☐ FOR YOUR INFORMATION

☐ RESPOND

☐ PLEASE COMMENT

☐ OTHER _____

_____

_____

_____

_____

_____

_____

_____

_____

_____

_____

_____

_____

_____

_____

_____

_____

_____

_____

PHONE MEMO

Call for: _____ Date: _____ Time: _____ am pm

Call from: _____

Of company: _____

Phone Number: _____ / _____ - _____

Message: _____

_____

_____

_____

Taken by: _____

Circle applicable response

Please call

Phoned

Returned your call

Will call again

PHONE MEMO

Call for: _____ Date: _____ Time: _____ am pm

Call from: _____

Of company: _____

Phone Number: _____ / _____ - _____

Message: _____

_____

_____

_____

Taken by: _____

Circle applicable response

Please call

Phoned

Returned your call

Will call again

INCOMING PHONE LOG

Date	Time	Call for	Call from	Of	Message	Please call	Will call again	Returned your call

OUTGOING PHONE LOG

Date	Length of call	Employee	Department	Person called	Company	City	Area code	Telephone number

MEMO-RESPONSE

FROM:

TO:

Date ____ / ____ / ____   Regarding

MEMO	RESPONSE

BY _____   SIGNED _____

ROUTING LABEL

Material ID:

Date: / /

Route to: _____

_____

_____

_____

_____

_____

Examine and pass on to next name on list.

ROUTING LABEL

Material ID:

Date: / /

Route to: _____

_____

_____

_____

_____

Examine and pass on to next name on list.

ROUTING LABEL

Material ID:

Date: / /

Route to: _____

_____

_____

_____

_____

Examine and pass on to next name on list.

ROUTING LABEL

Material ID:

Date: / /

Route to: _____

_____

_____

_____

_____

Examine and pass on to next name on list.

ITEMS NEEDED

Date submitted: / /

Date needed: / /

Submitted by: _____

Destination: _____

Attention: _____

Item/description	Quantity	Price per	Price	Date needed

Specifications/Suppliers to contact

TOTAL COST

ITEMS NEEDED

Date submitted: / /

Date needed: / /

Submitted by: _____

Destination: _____

Attention: _____

Item/description	Quantity	Price per	Price	Date needed

Specifications/Suppliers to contact

TOTAL COST

CHECK REQUEST

Date: ___ / ___ / ___

Needed by: _____

Department/Address: _____

Explanation:
```



```

Authorized by: _____

Received by: _____

Department/Title: _____

Amount sought: $ _____

Amount authorized: $ _____

Account number: _____

Check number: _____

Date: ___ / ___ / ___

CHECK REQUEST

Date: ___ / ___ / ___

Needed by: _____

Department/Address: _____

Explanation:
```



```

Authorized by: _____

Received by: _____

Department/Title: _____

Amount sought: $ _____

Amount authorized: $ _____

Account number: _____

Check number: _____

Date: ___ / ___ / ___

CHAPTER 11

Personnel Records:
Information required by law

A business with even one employee cannot operate without detailed personnel records. The law requires all employers, no matter how small, to maintain complete and separate records for each employee, including a *W-4 form*, an *employment eligibility verification form*, and thorough records of wages and payroll taxes paid and withheld. Forms provided to help you assemble and summarize this information include: *weekly time sheet; employee time sheet; payroll record; group payroll record; wage report; employee attendance record; quarterly payroll record/deductions;* and *quarterly payroll record/wages.* Stiff penalties can be incurred for not maintaining these records.

With today's increased litigation and unemployment insurance liabilities, employers need to take extreme care in firing employees. One step to reduce the possibility of an unjustified lawsuit is to document a problem employee's performance with such forms as the *employee absentee report* and the *employee warning notice* before firing an employee.

Of course, the best way to avoid problem employees is to hire excellent workers in the first place. Our detailed *employment application* can help you evaluate a job candidate carefully before making a hiring decision.

Remember that government agencies have little tolerance for even small employers that do not keep employee records. For example, if a previous employee makes a claim for unemployment insurance, the unemployment office will not even listen to an employer's opinion unless the employer can first promptly provide complete gross wage information, exact hiring date and exact final work date.

INDIVIDUAL PERSONNEL RECORD

Name: _____ Employee # _____

Address: _____

City: _____ State: _____ Zip: _____

Phone: /   -

Dates of Employment: From _____ to _____

Date(s) entered in file:

❑ Application
_____

❑ Resume
_____

❑ References
_____

Required Tax Forms:

_____   _____

_____   _____

_____   _____

_____   _____

❑ Attendance Record
_____

❑ Wage Report
_____

❑ Advance Request
_____

❑ Absentee Report
_____

❑ Warning Notice
_____

EMPLOYEE ROSTER

Name   Address   Phone

_____   _____   _____

_____   _____   _____

_____   _____   _____

_____   _____   _____

_____   _____   _____

_____   _____   _____

_____   _____   _____

_____   _____   _____

_____   _____   _____

_____   _____   _____

_____   _____   _____

_____   _____   _____

_____   _____   _____

_____   _____   _____

_____   _____   _____

_____   _____   _____

_____   _____   _____

_____   _____   _____

_____   _____   _____

_____   _____   _____

_____   _____   _____

_____   _____   _____

_____   _____   _____

_____   _____   _____

GROUP ATTENDANCE RECORD

Date   /   /

Name	In	Arrived Late (specify)	Left Early (specify)	Vacation Day	Sick/Personal Day

GROUP TIME SHEET

Date   /   /

NAME	MORNING		AFTERNOON		OFFICE USE ONLY	
	IN	OUT	IN	OUT	REGULAR HOURS	OVERTIME HOURS

NEW EMPLOYEE EVALUATION SURVEY

Name: _____

Day 1 . . . Excellent   Very Good   Good   Average   Below Average   Needs Improvement
Comments _____
_____

Day 2 . . . Excellent   Very Good   Good   Average   Below Average   Needs Improvement
Comments _____
_____

Day 3 . . . Excellent   Very Good   Good   Average   Below Average   Needs Improvement
Comments _____
_____

Day 4 . . . Excellent   Very Good   Good   Average   Below Average   Needs Improvement
Comments _____
_____

Day 5 . . . Excellent   Very Good   Good   Average   Below Average   Needs Improvement
Comments _____
_____

Day 6 . . . Excellent   Very Good   Good   Average   Below Average   Needs Improvement
Comments _____
_____

Day 7 . . . Excellent   Very Good   Good   Average   Below Average   Needs Improvement
Comments _____
_____

Day 8 . . . Excellent   Very Good   Good   Average   Below Average   Needs Improvement
Comments _____
_____

Day 9 . . . Excellent   Very Good   Good   Average   Below Average   Needs Improvement
Comments _____
_____

Day 10 . . Excellent   Very Good   Good   Average   Below Average   Needs Improvement
Comments _____

Name: _____ Year: _____

JAN . . . . Excellent   Very Good   Good   Average   Below Average   Needs Improvement
(circle one)   Comments _____

FEB . . . . Excellent   Very Good   Good   Average   Below Average   Needs Improvement
Comments _____

MAR . . . Excellent   Very Good   Good   Average   Below Average   Needs Improvement
Comments _____

APR . . . Excellent   Very Good   Good   Average   Below Average   Needs Improvement
Comments _____

MAY . . . Excellent   Very Good   Good   Average   Below Average   Needs Improvement
Comments _____

JUN . . . Excellent   Very Good   Good   Average   Below Average   Needs Improvement
Comments _____

JUL . . . . Excellent   Very Good   Good   Average   Below Average   Needs Improvement
Comments _____

AUG . . . Excellent   Very Good   Good   Average   Below Average   Needs Improvement
Comments _____

SEP . . . . Excellent   Very Good   Good   Average   Below Average   Needs Improvement
Comments _____

OCT . . . Excellent   Very Good   Good   Average   Below Average   Needs Improvement
Comments _____

NOV . . . Excellent   Very Good   Good   Average   Below Average   Needs Improvement
Comments _____

DEC . . . Excellent   Very Good   Good   Average   Below Average   Needs Improvement
Comments _____

WEEKLY TIME SHEET

FROM   /   /   TO   /   /

Name _____   No. ____

Department _____

	MORNING		AFTERNOON		FOR OFFICE USE ONLY	
	IN	OUT	IN	OUT	REGULAR HOURS	OVERTIME HOURS
MONDAY						
TUESDAY						
WEDNESDAY						
THURSDAY						
FRIDAY						
SATURDAY						
SUNDAY						

Signature _____   TOTAL HOURS

WEEKLY TIME SHEET

FROM   /   /   TO   /   /

Name _____   No. ____

Department _____

	MORNING		AFTERNOON		FOR OFFICE USE ONLY	
	IN	OUT	IN	OUT	REGULAR HOURS	OVERTIME HOURS
MONDAY						
TUESDAY						
WEDNESDAY						
THURSDAY						
FRIDAY						
SATURDAY						
SUNDAY						

Signature _____   TOTAL HOURS

EMPLOYEE TIME SHEET

FROM   /   /   TO   /   /

Name _____   No. ____

Department _____

DATE	MORNING		AFTERNOON		FOR OFFICE USE ONLY	
	IN	OUT	IN	OUT	REGULAR HOURS	OVERTIME HOURS

TOTAL HOURS

Signature _____

PAYROLL RECORD

PERSON	HOURLY RATE	WEEKLY RATE	ANNUAL RATE

Gross payroll costs: _____

Employer's share of payroll taxes: _____

Total payroll costs: _____

GROUP PAYROLL RECORD

Date from   /   /

Date to   /   /

EMPLOYEE	EXEMPTIONS	HOURS WORKED		RATE	WAGE/SALARY		TOTAL WAGES PAID
		Regular	Overtime		Regular	Overtime	

TOTAL WAGES PAID/GROUP

WAGE REPORT

Employee: _____

Soc. Sec. Number: _____

Period from: ___ / ___ / ___

to: ___ / ___ / ___

INCOME

	# HOURS	RATE	TOTAL
Regular hours:	___	___	___
Overtime hours:	___	___	___
Vacation:	___	___	___
	___	___	___

GROSS EARNINGS _____

DEDUCTIONS

Social Security (FICA): _____

Federal witholding tax: _____

State witholding tax: _____

Local witholding tax: _____

Other: _____

TOTAL DEDUCTIONS _____

NET WAGES _____

KEEP THIS STATEMENT FOR YOUR RECORDS

WAGE REPORT

Employee: _____

Soc. Sec. Number: _____

Period from: ___ / ___ / ___

to: ___ / ___ / ___

INCOME

	# HOURS	RATE	TOTAL
Regular hours:	___	___	___
Overtime hours:	___	___	___
Vacation:	___	___	___
	___	___	___

GROSS EARNINGS _____

DEDUCTIONS

Social Security (FICA): _____

Federal witholding tax: _____

State witholding tax: _____

Local witholding tax: _____

Other: _____

TOTAL DEDUCTIONS _____

NET WAGES _____

KEEP THIS STATEMENT FOR YOUR RECORDS

EMPLOYEE ATTENDANCE RECORD

For Year   19

Name _____

Employee Number _____

Soc. Sec. Number _____

	JAN	FEB	MAR	APR	MAY	JUN	JUL	AUG	SEP	OCT	NOV	DEC
1												
2												
3												
4												
5												
6												
7												
8												
9												
10												
11												
12												
13												
14												
15												
16												
17												
18												
19												
20												
21												
22												
23												
24												
25												
26												
27												
28												
29												
30												
31												

Attendance Codes

X   (Excused Absence)

V   (Vacation)   JD   (Jury Duty)

S   (Sick)   UA   (Unexcused Absence)

QUARTERLY PAYROLL RECORD/WAGES

Employee name: _____

Employee number: _____

Quarter Number: 1   2   3   4

WEEK ENDING	HOURS									RATE	WAGES		TOTAL WAGES
	S	M	T	W	T	F	S	Reg	O.T.		Regular	Overtime	

QUARTERLY TOTALS

QUARTERLY PAYROLL RECORD/WAGES

Employee name: _____

Employee number: _____

Quarter Number: 1   2   3   4

WEEK ENDING	HOURS									RATE	WAGES		TOTAL WAGES
	S	M	T	W	T	F	S	Reg	O.T.		Regular	Overtime	

QUARTERLY TOTALS

QUARTERLY PAYROLL RECORD/DEDUCTIONS

Employee name: _____

Employee number: _____

Quarter Number: 1   2   3   4

DEDUCTIONS							NET PAY	CHECK NUMBER
Social Security	Withholding Taxes			Insurance				
	Federal	State	Local					

QUARTERLY PAYROLL RECORD/DEDUCTIONS

Employee name: _____

Employee number: _____

Quarter Number: 1   2   3   4

DEDUCTIONS							NET PAY	CHECK NUMBER
Social Security	Withholding Taxes			Insurance				
	Federal	State	Local					

EMPLOYEE ABSENTEE REPORT

NAME _____ DATE ___ / ___ / ___

DEPARTMENT _____

CIRCLE REASON	WAS ABSENT FROM WORK TODAY
SICK	REMARKS (Please be specific)
VACATION	
PERMISSION	
UNKNOWN	
OTHER	
_____	
_____	
_____	

SIGNATURE OF SUPERVISOR _____ OFFICIAL SIGNATURE _____

EMPLOYEE ABSENTEE REPORT

NAME _____ DATE ___ / ___ / ___

DEPARTMENT _____

CIRCLE REASON	WAS ABSENT FROM WORK TODAY
SICK	REMARKS (Please be specific)
VACATION	
PERMISSION	
UNKNOWN	
OTHER	
_____	
_____	
_____	

SIGNATURE OF SUPERVISOR _____ OFFICIAL SIGNATURE _____

EMPLOYEE WARNING NOTICE

1st Notice
2nd Notice

NAME _____   DATE ___/___/___

DEPARTMENT _____

VIOLATION

LATE ARRIVAL

EARLY DEPARTURE

ABSENT

ATTITUDE

SAFETY VIOLATION

DEFECTIVE WORK

OTHER

_____

_____

REMARKS
(Please be
specific) _____

_____

_____

_____

_____

_____

_____

_____

SIGNATURE OF SUPERVISOR _____   OFFICIAL SIGNATURE _____

EMPLOYEE WARNING NOTICE

1st Notice
2nd Notice

NAME _____   DATE ___/___/___

DEPARTMENT _____

VIOLATION

LATE ARRIVAL

EARLY DEPARTURE

ABSENT

ATTITUDE

SAFETY VIOLATION

DEFECTIVE WORK

OTHER

_____

_____

REMARKS
(Please be
specific) _____

_____

_____

_____

_____

_____

_____

_____

SIGNATURE OF SUPERVISOR _____   OFFICIAL SIGNATURE _____

159

EMPLOYMENT APPLICATION

(Please print)

Date of application: _____ / _____ / _____

Position(s) applied for: _____

How did you hear about this position?
(please circle)

| Advertisement | Friend | Relative | Walk-in |
| Employment Agency | Other _____ | | |

Name _____

LAST   FIRST   MIDDLE

Address _____

NUMBER   STREET   CITY   STATE   ZIP

Telephone _____ / _____ - _____

Social Security No. _____

Please circle response.

If employed and under 18, can you furnish a work permit?	Yes	No
Have you applied for work here before?	Yes	No
If "Yes", give date _____		
Have you even been employed here before?	Yes	No
If "Yes", give date _____		
Are you employed now?	Yes	No
May we contact your present employer?	Yes	No
Are you prevented from lawfully becoming employed in this country because of Vias or Immigration Status?	Yes	No
(Proof of citizenship or immigration status will be required upon employment)		
On what date would you be available to work?	_____ / _____ / _____	
Please circle the category that best summarizes your available hours:	Full-time Part-time	
	Shift work Temporary	
Can you travel if a job requires it?	Yes	No
Are you on a lay-off and subject to recall?	Yes	No
Have you been convicted of a felony within the last 5 years?	Yes	No
If "Yes", please explain _____		
Are you a veteran of the U.S. Military?	Yes	No
If "Yes", specify branch _____		
Was your discharge other than honorable?	Yes	No
If "Yes", please explain _____		

Education

	HIGH SCHOOL	COLLEGE/UNIV.	GRADUATE/PROF.
School name, location			
Years Completed/Degree			
Diploma/Degree			
Describe Course Of Study			
Outline specialized training, apprenticeships, internships, skills and extra-curricular activities			

Honors Received: State any additional information you feel may be helpful to us in considering your application. If necessary, please use a separate sheet of paper.

List professional, trade, business or civic activities and offices held. **(You may exclude memberships which would reveal sex, race, religion, national origin, age, ancestry, or handicap or other proctected status.):**

_____

_____

_____

Please list the name, address and daytime telephone number of three references who are not related to you and are not previous employers.

_____

_____

_____

Briefly summarize special skills and qualifications you have acquired from your employment or other experience.

_____

_____

_____

Do you speak a foreign language? If so, note below; please list your ability to read and write in that language

_____

_____

Employment History

Please give an accurate, complete employment record, filling out all sections Start with your present or last job. Include military service assignments and volunteer activities. You may exclude organization names which may disclose your race, religion, color, national origin, gender, handicap, or other protected status.

Employer	Telephone ( )	Dates Employed		Work Performed
		From	To	
Address				
Job Title		Hourly Rate/Salary		
		Starting	Final	
Supervisor				
Reason for Leaving				
Employer	Telephone ( )	Dates Employed		Work Performed
		From	To	
Address				
Job Title		Hourly Rate/Salary		
		Starting	Final	
Supervisor				
Reason for Leaving				
Employer	Telephone ( )	Dates Employed		Work Performed
		From	To	
Address				
Job Title		Hourly Rate/Salary		
		Starting	Final	
Supervisor				
Reason for Leaving				

If you need additional space, please continue on a separate sheet of paper.

Signature

The information provided in this Employment Application is true, correct and complete. If employed, any misstatement or omission of fact on this application may result in my dismissal.

I authorize you to engage a consumer reporting agency to investigate my credit and personal history. If a report is obtained you must provide, at my request, the name and address of the agency so I may obtain from them the nature and substance of the report.

I understand that an offer of employment does not create a contractual obligation upon the employer to continue to employ me in the future.

_____   _____
Date   Signature

EMPLOYEE SEPARATION NOTICE

NAME _____   DATE ___ / ___ / ___

DEPARTMENT _____

CIRCLE REASON
LACK OF WORK
SICK
ABSENCE
INJURY
DEATH
RETIRED
QUIT
OTHER
_____

LEFT OUR EMPLOY TODAY

REMARKS
(Please be specific)

_____

_____

_____

_____

_____

_____

SIGNATURE OF SUPERVISOR _____   OFFICIAL SIGNATURE _____

EMPLOYEE SEPARATION NOTICE

NAME _____   DATE ___ / ___ / ___

DEPARTMENT _____

CIRCLE REASON
LACK OF WORK
SICK
ABSENCE
INJURY
DEATH
RETIRED
QUIT
OTHER
_____

LEFT OUR EMPLOY TODAY

REMARKS
(Please be specific)

_____

_____

_____

_____

_____

_____

SIGNATURE OF SUPERVISOR _____   OFFICIAL SIGNATURE _____

ADVANCE REQUEST

Date   /   /

Amount desired: _____   For: _____

Amount authorized: _____   Approved by: _____

Check/Voucher #: _____   Title/Department: _____

Explanation:

Signed: _____

ADVANCE REQUEST

Date   /   /

Amount desired: _____   For: _____

Amount authorized: _____   Approved by: _____

Check/Voucher #: _____   Title/Department: _____

Explanation:

Signed: _____

CHAPTER 12

Result Trackers:

Forms that evaluate your performance

The forms in this section are essential for preparing a tax return, and are also vital for evaluating the performance and well-being of your business.

Your income tax forms will be very similar to the *profit and loss statement*. If your business is incorporated, you will also need to submit a beginning- and end-of-year balance sheet similar to the *corporate balance sheet form*.

While the profit and loss statement is an important gauge of the success and health of a business, the *balance sheet* is generally a better indicator. For example, a business might show a huge profit on the profit and loss statement -- but if the profit is tied up in bad debt and excess inventory then the business might be experiencing cash flow difficulty which could lead to bankruptcy. That is why banks and other lenders place particular importance on balance sheets. You should too. Keep a careful eye to see if receivables and inventories are growing faster than sales.

If your business is not incorporated, banks will want to see the *individual/partnership balance sheet*. If the balance sheet for your partnership reflects only business assets, the bank will also want to see personal balance sheets from all partners. If your business is incorporated but somewhat smaller than General Motors, the bank will want to see a personal balance sheet in addition to the corporate balance sheet and will almost certainly ask you to personally guarantee any loans.

Trade creditors will often ask for a copy of your balance sheet but, unlike the bank, seldom ask for a copy of your Income Statement.

The *profit and loss variance form* helps you pinpoint areas in which you may be able to cut costs by showing you the difference from one year (or month) to the next.

The *straight-line depreciation form* helps you calculate depreciation for tax purposes and for creating your balance sheet.

While the number of forms in this section is not large, these forms are fundamental business tools that you should refer to frequently. In fact, in many instances you will benefit by assembling and examining a profit and loss statement or a balance sheet every month!

PROFIT & LOSS STATEMENT

Year: _____

INCOME

Gross sales:	_____
Less returns:	_____
Less bad debt:	_____
Interest, rent, royalty income:	_____
TOTAL INCOME	[ ]

EXPENSES

Cost of goods sold:	_____
Direct payroll:	_____
Indirect payroll:	_____
Taxes, other than income tax:	_____
Sales expenses:	_____
Shipping, postage:	_____
Advertising, promotion:	_____
Office expenses:	_____
Travel, entertainment:	_____
Phone:	_____
Other utilities:	_____
Auto/truck:	_____
Insurance:	_____
Professional fees:	_____
Rent:	_____
Interest on loans:	_____
Other:	_____
TOTAL EXPENSES BEFORE TAX	[ ]
NET INCOME	[ ]
INCOME TAX	_____
NET INCOME AFTER TAX	[ ]

CORPORATE BALANCE SHEET

ASSETS

Cash: _____

Accounts receivable: _____

Less bad debt allowance: _____

Inventory: _____

Loan to stockholders: _____

Depreciable, depletable and intangible assets: _____

Less accumulated depreciations,
depletion and amortization: _____

Other assets: _____

TOTAL ASSETS _____

LIABILITIES

Accounts payable: _____

Taxes: _____

Other current liabilities: _____

Loans from stockholders: _____

Mortgages, notes, bonds payable: _____

Other liabilities: _____

Capital Stock: _____

Paid-in or capital surplus: _____

Retained earnings: _____

Less cost of treasury stock: _____

TOTAL LIABILITIES
AND STOCKHOLDER'S EQUITY _____

BALANCE SHEET
INDIVIDUAL/PARTNERSHIP

ASSETS

Cash: _____

Accounts receivable: _____

Less bad debt allowance: _____

Inventory: _____

Loan to partners, key employees: _____

Depreciable, depletable and intangible
assets: _____

Less accumulated depreciations,
depletion and amortization: _____

Real estate: _____

Other assets: _____

TOTAL ASSETS _____

LIABILITIES

Accounts payable: _____

Taxes: _____

Other current liabilities: _____

Loans: _____

Mortgages, notes, bonds payable: _____

Net worth: _____

TOTAL LIABILITIES _____

PROFIT & LOSS VARIANCE

Year: _____

or Month: _____

	Previous Year	Estimate	Actual	Difference	Percent Difference
Gross sales:					
Less returns:					
Less bad debt:					
Interest, rent, royalty income:					
TOTAL INCOME					
EXPENSES					
Cost of goods sold:					
Direct payroll:					
Indirect payroll:					
Taxes, other than income tax:					
Sales expenses:					
Shipping, postage:					
Advertising, promotion:					
Office expenses:					
Travel, entertainment:					
Phone:					
Other utilities:					
Auto/truck:					
Insurance:					
Professional fees:					
Rent:					
Interest on loans:					
Other:					
TOTAL EXPENSES BEFORE TAX					
NET INCOME					
INCOME TAX					
NET INCOME AFTER TAX					

STRAIGHT-LINE DEPRECIATION SCHEDULE

Item/ description	Date placed in service	Total cost paid	Depreciation recovery period	Total depreciation	Annual depreciation	Depreciation time	
						From	To

TOTAL DEPRECIATION

Prepared by: _____

Date _____ / _____ / _____

CHAPTER 13

Business Growers:
Forms that plan the future

By planning your business future carefully you can increase your profits, build confidence with your banker, and foresee any cash flow problems long before they occur.

It is extremely important in the *pro forma profit and loss projection* to assume differing levels of sales. It is impossible to ever project sales precisely, but it is usually possible to project sales fairly accurately within a range. Then, assuming different sales levels, you should plan to adjust your expenses accordingly to maintain the best possible profit margin. In making a presentation to a bank, you will want to show at least three different assumptions for levels of sales.

Interestingly, the very time that your business experiences strong sales and fast growth is the time it can very likely run out of cash and credit. This is because receivables and inventory will normally increase even faster than sales. So, if you are planning for your business to grow quickly (and who isn't?) you need to plan your future cash needs very carefully.

The *pro forma cash flow* will help you project your receipt of cash and your disbursement of cash to determine net cash needs. Be sure to project receipt of invoices realistically for vendors of your size in your industry, which will probably be after your stated terms. Remember as you establish credit with your vendors that you will be able to stretch out payments to the industry standard time.

The *five-year balance sheet* will also be useful for planning cash flow for the future. Key variables are accounts receivable, cash and inventory. Although your bank might be willing to meet your initial seasonal accounts receivable financing needs, they might not be willing to increase the financing as quickly as you are planning to increase your accounts receivable.

If you really want to see your small business grow significantly, you will succeed much more easily if you plan your growth in advance.

PRO-FORMA PROFIT & LOSS

Year: _____

or Month: _____

	Previous Year	Sales Scenarios		
		WEAK	LIKELY	GOOD
INCOME				
Gross sales:				
Less returns:				
Less bad debt:				
Interest, rent, royalty income:				
TOTAL INCOME				
EXPENSES				
Cost of goods sold:				
Direct payroll:				
Indirect payroll:				
Taxes, other than income tax:				
Sales expenses:				
Shipping, postage:				
Advertising, promotion:				
Office expenses:				
Travel, entertainment:				
Phone:				
Other utilities:				
Auto/truck:				
Insurance:				
Professional fees:				
Rent:				
Interest on loans:				
Other:				
TOTAL EXPENSES BEFORE TAX				
NET INCOME				
INCOME TAX				
NET INCOME AFTER TAX				

PRO-FORMA CASH FLOW

	JAN	FEB	MAR	APR	MAY	JUN	JUL	AUG	SEP	OCT	NOV	DEC
INFLOW												
Cash on hand beginning of month:												
From sales:												
From interest, etc.:												
Loan proceeds:												
Inflow plus cash on hand:												
OUTFLOW												
Cost of goods sold:												
Direct payroll:												
Indirect payroll:												
Taxes, other than income tax:												
Sales expenses:												
Shipping, postage:												
Advertising, promotion:												
Office expenses:												
Travel, entertainment:												
Phone:												
Other utilities:												
Auto/truck:												
Insurance:												
Professional fees:												
Rent:												
Interest on loans:												
Taxes:												
Loan pay-down:												
Other:												
Cash outflow subtotal:												
Net cash on hand, end of month:												

5-YEAR PRO-FORMA CASH FLOW

	YEAR #1	YEAR #2	YEAR #3	YEAR #4	YEAR #5
INFLOW					
Cash on hand beginning of year:					
From sales:					
From interest, etc.:					
Loan proceeds:					
Inflow plus cash on hand:	___	___	___	___	___
OUTFLOW					
Cost of goods sold:					
Direct payroll:					
Indirect payroll:					
Taxes, other than income tax:					
Sales expenses:					
Shipping, postage:					
Advertising, promotion:					
Office expenses:					
Travel, entertainment:					
Phone:					
Other utilities:					
Auto/truck:					
Insurance:					
Professional fees:					
Rent:					
Interest on loans:					
Taxes:					
Loan pay-down:					
Other:					
Cash outflow subtotal:	___	___	___	___	___
Cash on hand, end of year:	___	___	___	___	___

5-YEAR BALANCE SHEET PLANNER

	Year _____	Year _____	Year _____	Year _____	Year _____
ASSETS					
Cash					
Accounts receivable					
Less bad debt allowance					
Inventory					
Loan to stockholders					
Depreciable, depletable and intangible assets					
Less accumulated depreciation, depletion and amortization					
Other assets					
TOTAL ASSETS					
LIABILITIES					
Accounts payable					
Taxes					
Other liabilities					
Loans from stockholders					
Mortgages, notes, bonds payable					
Other liabilities					
Capital stock					
Paid-in or capital surplus					
Retained earnings					
Less cost of treasury stock					
TOTAL LIABILITIES AND STOCKHOLDER'S EQUITY					

PRO-FORMA PAYROLL COSTS

PERSON	HOURLY RATE	WEEKLY RATE	ANNUAL RATE

Gross payroll costs: _____

Employer's share of payroll taxes: _____

Total payroll costs: _____

BUSINESS START-UP CASH NEEDS

Basic one-time costs

Real estate deposit:	_____
Phone deposit:	_____
Other utility deposits:	_____
Rent before opening:	_____
Phone before opening:	_____
Other utilities before opening:	_____
Payroll before opening:	_____
Remodeling costs:	_____
Equipment costs:	_____
Fixtures, furniture, signs:	_____
Legal fees:	_____
Accounting fees:	_____

Subtotal [   ]

Starting inventory/raw goods

Detail:_____   _____

_____   _____

_____   _____

Subtotal [   ]

Initial advertising/promotion

Detail:_____   _____

_____   _____

_____   _____

Subtotal [   ]

Reserve for _____ months' operating expenses

Detail:_____   _____

_____   _____

_____   _____

Subtotal [   ]

TOTAL [   ]

CHAPTER 14

Blank Grids & Charts:
Customize your own forms

If you have use for a particular form and none of the many forms in this book are appropriate, you can easily create a good-looking form by using the blank forms on the following pages.

Make your own forms as attractive as possible by entering headlines with a typewriter. Another alternative is to paste a label, with your desired headline, over the existing headlines on the finished forms in this book.

While the forms in this book will solve most of your business needs, you should be able to customize the grids and charts on the following pages for virtually any other use.

Remember, with TEN-SECOND BUSINESS FORMS it only takes seconds to look professional!

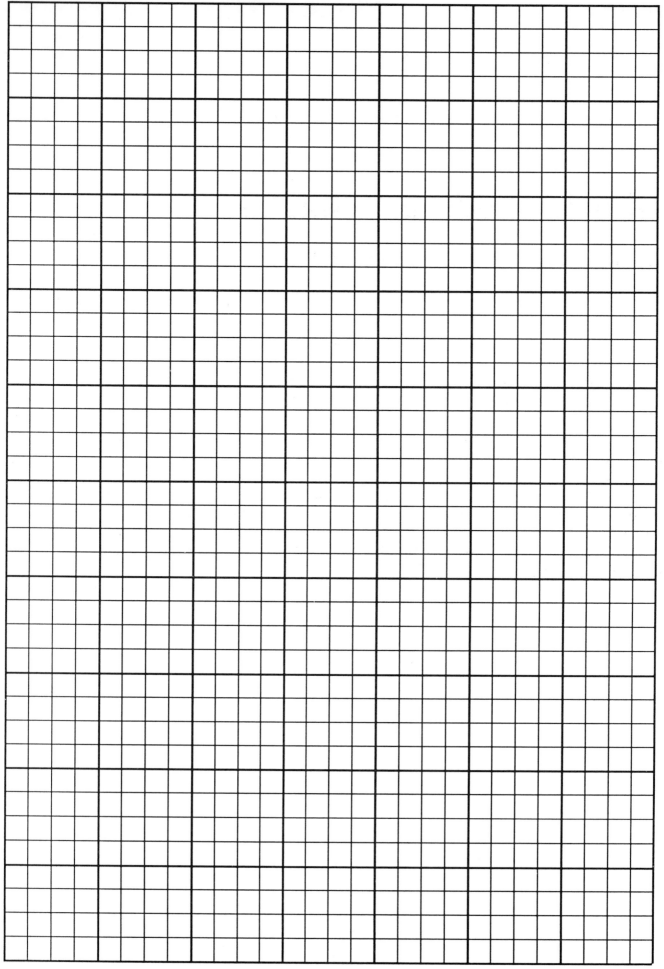

GRID: 1/4" x 1/4"

GRID: 1/10" x 1/10"

184

GRID: 1-1/2" x 1/4"

GRID: 1" x 1/4" with 1" column head

GRID: 1" x 1/4" with 1" column head

GRID: 1 1/2" x 1/2" with 1" column head

GRID: 1 1/2" x 1/4" with 1" column heads and total boxes

GRID: 1" x 1/4"

GRID: 2" x 1/4"

GRID: 2-1/4" x 1/4"

GRID: 1" x 1/4" with 1" column heads

GRID: 1 1/4" x 1/4" with 1" column heads

GRID: 1 1/4" x 1/4" with 1" column heads and total boxes

GRID: 1 1/2" x 1/4" with 1" column heads and total boxes

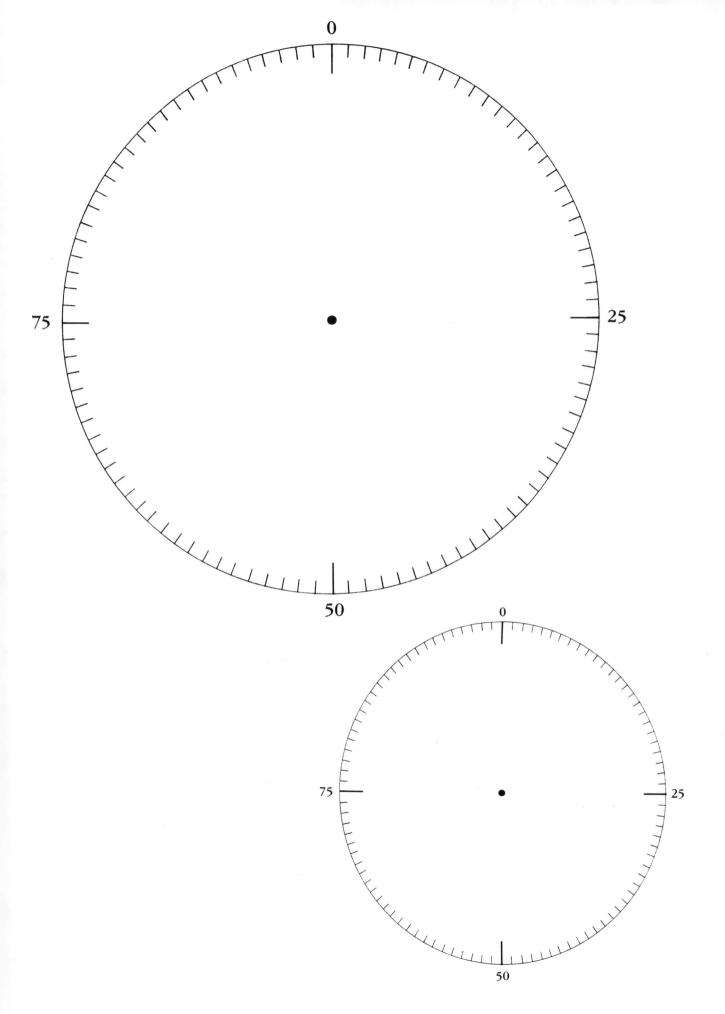

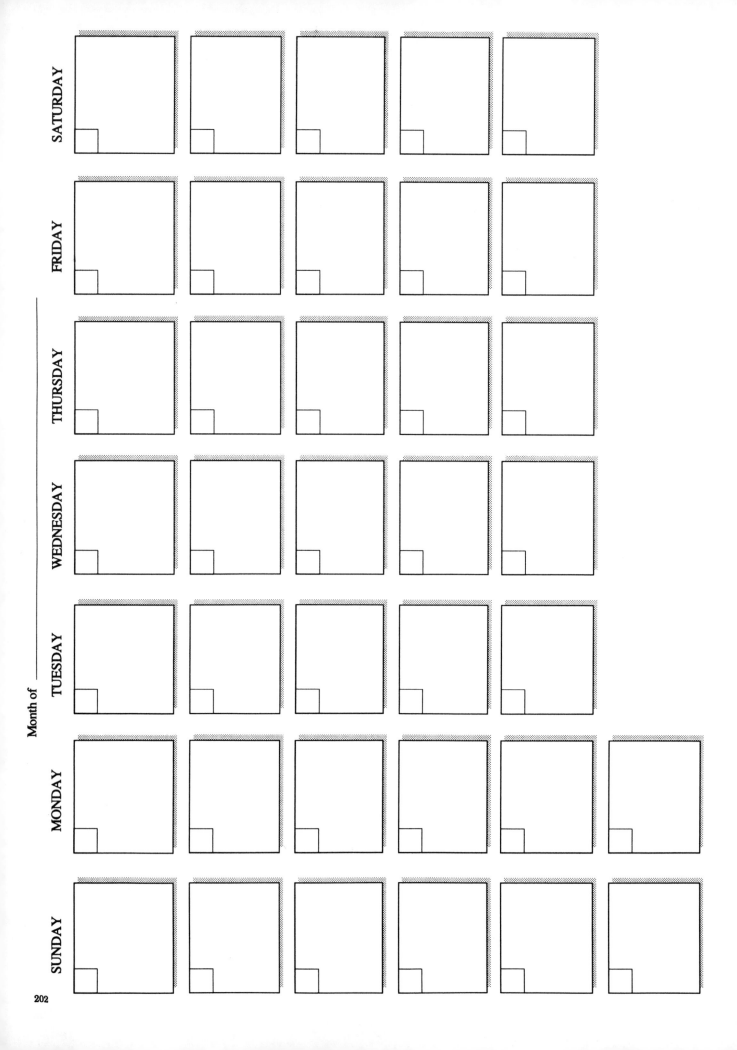

SATURDAY

FRIDAY

THURSDAY

WEDNESDAY

TUESDAY

MONDAY

SUNDAY

Month of _____

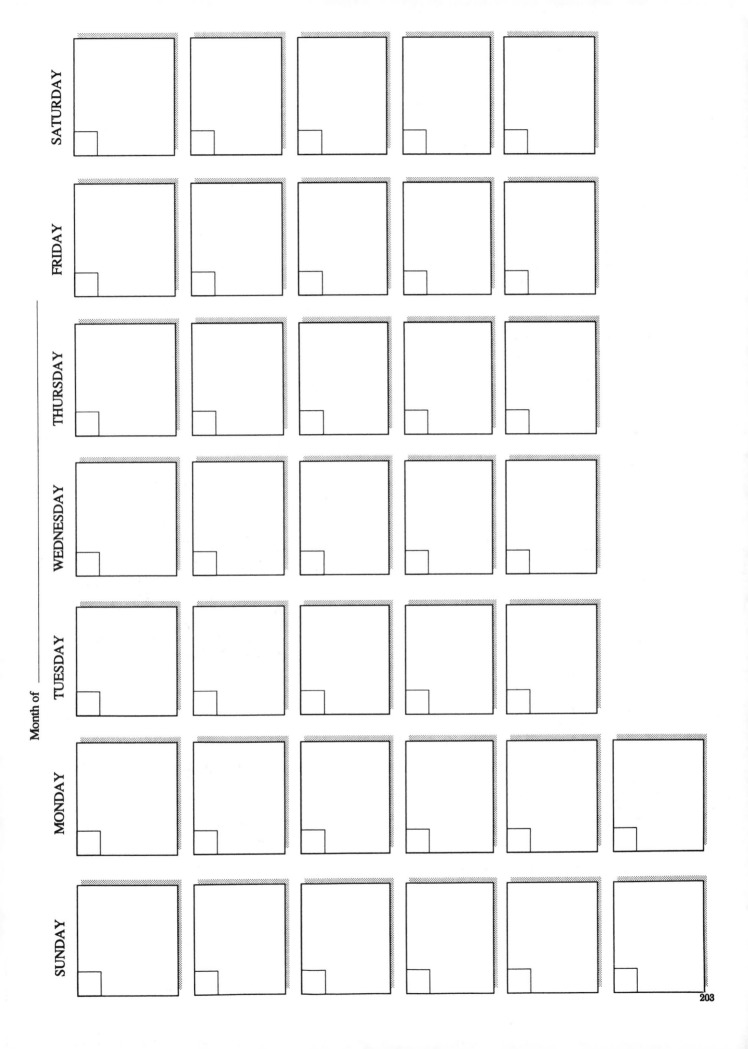

SATURDAY

FRIDAY

THURSDAY

WEDNESDAY

TUESDAY

MONDAY

SUNDAY

Index

a

b

c

d

e

About the Author:

Robert L. Adams has a broad background in operating a number of small businesses - *all of which would have benefited tremendously from the forms in Ten-Second Business Forms.* He has owned and successfully operated: a house painting business, a bicycle rental business, a boat brokerage firm, a tourist map business, a phone directory business, a college newspaper, and a classified advertising newspaper.

Currently, Adams is the President of Bob Adams, Inc., a multi-million dollar international publishing firm that he founded eight years ago.

Adams is a graduate of the Harvard Business School, where he received first-year honors. He received his BA from Carleton College.

Adams has applied his diversified business background to the design of Ten-Second Business Forms, making it an extremely useful tool for all small businesses.